Dan Holdsworth

Dan Holdsworth
Spatial Objects

DISTANZ

Alistair Robinson

Temporal Subjects

To start at the beginning, the title *Spatial Objects* is wilfully misleading – at least in one sense. The title derives from a term in computer programming used to designate objects that exist, as Holdsworth notes, "in simultaneous symmetry within the virtual and the real". The starting points for *Spatial Objects*, despite their appearance as marking a departure from Holdsworth's work to date, were the digitally recorded GPS points harvested in the production of an earlier series. The 'image', if we can call it that, is in fact ultimately derived from US Geological Survey mapping data of Crater Lake, in the western United States, and part of a protected National Park. (There is one exception: the artist's own data take from a glacier in the French Alps, that is part of the Mont Blanc massif.)

In this sense, the images we encounter are the literal code – let us call it the pictorial 'DNA' for now – from which the artist's previous series of work was derived. We have returned to source, as it were, to individual instances of 'raw data' expanded to fill our field of vision, to become the object of our attention. The works raise the obvious question of what it is we are actually looking at, but they also invite us to reflect on the nature of our looking, and how it is conditioned in the early twenty-first century. The 'what' is both simple to describe and impossible to fully conceptualise. Each image is drawn from what the artist describes as "a geographical 3D virtual landscape composed of data depicting the architectural geometry of individual 3D pixels – or more accurately, small fragmented parts of 3D pixels which themselves also represent coordinate points."

The dramatic departure in *Spatial Objects*, away from Holdsworth's previous work is the continuation of his investigations on an entirely different scale, working from the macro towards micro. Several of his previous works, from the earliest urban landscapes such as *A Machine for Living* (1999–2000), to *Megalith* (2000–2) present us with alarming and alluring man-made environments. In both we encounter expansive vistas that appear as strangely virtualised or interchangeable 'non-places', as theorised by Marc Augé (1995). Certainly Holdsworth is well aware of the artistic and photographic predecessors who have called into question the intrinsically ennobling effects of encountering the 'landscape', such as those associated with the exhibition New Topographics (1976). Like the photography of Bernd and Hilla Becher, both these early series of Holdsworth's work offer images of built 'spaces' rather than 'places'. A third series offers the teasing title *The World in Itself* (2000–1) and here the works make manifest their status as representations in a similar way to Andreas Gursky's landscapes. 'Nature' takes on peculiar qualities of regularity and symmetry, and (human) presence is connoted precisely by its absence.

The spaces in all three series appear almost to have been computer-generated, certainly computer designed; that is, they are 'model spaces' brought to our attention via the imaginative pathways they offer through an idea of twenty-first century space. The spaces, even when tangible or tactile in their surfaces, bear a trace of their seemingly digital construction in their very materiality. (Or else in their absence of 'ordinary' materiality). In *Spatial Objects* this process might be described as having been reversed or turned inside out. Again, nothing is precisely what it seems. Rather, the virtual realm has become all too 'real' and made violently palpable – even quietly confrontational.

Many of Holdsworth's works have opened out an immeasurable vastness to the eye and offered novel and radical takes on eighteenth-century classical notions of the sublime offered by Edmund Burke and Immanuel Kant, amongst others. Perhaps most vividly, this line of enquiry can be seen in a series of five works entitled *Infinite Pictures*, made between 2006 and 2009. These works make literal their titles rather than offering counter-readings between image and text. Each is shot from an 'inhuman' viewpoint that we, the camera, would never have been able to occupy – a God's eye view over the world's most uninhabitable places (as opposed to spaces).

The series are, obviously, modern-day photographic versions of Caspar David Friedrich's High Romantic cloudscapes and seascapes but they also offer new insights that *Spatial Objects* alight from. Indeed it would be conceivable to imagine *Spatial Objects* retitled as Infinite Pictures. In both series, we encounter spaces, even whilst this appears a counter-intuitive reading apropos the newer work, and in both spaces, human presence and human agency are not only absent, but essentially an impossibility. Humans cannot and could not subsist in either the empty heavens above, or the virtual realm 'inside' our computer screens. Both are types of 'infinity', but made palpable. We might think of *Spatial Objects* as embodying a new form of infinity, as infinitely small objects held up for our attention so that we can begin to understand them.

Throughout Holdsworth's career, the devil has always been in the details, here just as much as earlier. What we encounter, in fact, are the 'edges' of pixels rendered in three dimensions; the shadowed areas are their contours. At this point, the process of bringing the virtual 'to life' reaches technological as well as conceptual limits. As he notes, "the edges are absolutes at the level of representation, but the rendering of the data at such a level of proximity to the individual GPS point within a virtual landscape creates a certain level of visual error." (There is a direct photographic parallel that can bring this to mind. It is as though we have 'zoomed in' too far, too fast, so that the computer's virtual lens can no longer focus, or properly process the image.)

The result of this creative misuse, or redirection of what are high-end technologies, allows us to make the technology and its operations themselves visible. One purpose of Holdsworth's experimental use of digital imaging software is "to make visible the 'interface' itself". The purpose of this, in turn, is to allow us to at least begin to examine the digital-imaging world we now all take for granted, but about which so little is understood. For Holdsworth, the world has become known and indeed knowable not only through images – that much has been true for centuries – but through 'computer architectures' that predetermine both the 'forms of knowledge' open to us, and the 'forms' in which knowledge is communicated. The observation that 'the medium is the message' has been a commonplace since first coined by Marshall McLuhan in 1964, at the very beginning of the computer age.

In *Spatial Objects*, the medium of artistic investigation is made the object of that investigation, and its objects are made opaque and knowable to us rather than being taken for granted, or seen as transparent in their effects and operations.

This investigation has its own, peculiar poetry, of course. Looking at *Spatial Objects* has been described as "like zooming in on the individual scales of a butterfly's wing" by critic Melanie Vandenbrouck. The glistening expanses of saturated, vivid colour remind us that the links between the 'luminous' and the 'numinous' is not merely phonetic.

Holdsworth is one of the very first artists to understand how this applies to a new environment in which almost every part of our world is instantly visible from our armchairs and desks through Google Earth. As he remarks, almost none of us are able to visualise or conceive of "the computer architectures that underpin our human/computer interactions and our contemporary experience of space through GPS mapping." And as he also remarks, "similar technologies are common to the construction of virtual landscapes in computer games, for cinema, and those in GPS mapping, available on every mobile phone or computer worldwide." The mass diffusion of and crossover between these technologies, allows anyone with a computer to build virtual spaces from anywhere on the globe. Similarly, they allow us to 'virtualise the global', to view the whole planet from a phone or laptop screen. Yet their workings remain beyond the reaches of our imagination; none of us could build a computer, let alone recreate the software to construct an entire virtual realm, especially if all prior examples are destroyed. The 'means of production' remain invisible to us: we have no ontology available to deal with them. When data took the form of mere numbers, this did not seem a pressing problem. When they took command of what Henri Lefebvre calls 'the production of space' – across both the production of knowledge about geographical space, and the production of virtual space – then we become ignorant of how our own knowledge is being shaped (Lefebvre, 1991).

Of course, our imbrication in such technologies scarcely ends there. Anyone owning a mobile phone is continually monitored and mapped by their service provider, as well as subject to satellite surveillance. One startling conclusion from a close reading of *Spatial Objects* is that they are 'portraits' not only of data points but also, by proxy, portraits of individuals – of us – as seen by a GPS handling computer. Each of us is just a signal to a GPS computer system, a mere 'data point' in Holdsworth's own words; one amongst tens of millions. Imagining the human species within any nation state as tens of millions of co-ordinates continually in motion, is of course as much a 'God's eye view' as that in Infinite Pictures. Indeed it is a dramatically original and potent re-envisioning of this idea; it remains beyond our ability to visualize or comprehend even whilst we can conceive of it, whilst being an entirely new image of the sublime. The serial nature of the work implies that it is inherently replicable and that we could, in theory, imagine sixty-million *Spatial Objects* infinitely aligned, that could document the entirety of Crater Lake, or the population of a nation.

Despite Holdsworth's ongoing fascination with remaking and rethinking the modern sublime, *Spatial Objects* marks one obvious and distinct departure from the rest of his twenty-year practice, in that we immediately attend to the specifically sculptural qualities of each work rather than that which is represented within the image alone (though this applies as well). Each of the larger objects in the series is above human height, and appear both oddly monumental and anti-monumental at the same time. The works might well be characterised by their impossibility to be characterised adequately – by which I mean that any adjectival description is either insufficient, or else immediately contradicted. It is difficult to locate them properly in our imaginations. Holdsworth's gift is to have found what T.S. Eliot called a poetic 'objective correlative' for the most micro scaled forms of data, that convinces us of its fidelity, and to deftly contradict what any clichéd image of 'data' might be connected to. Therefore each object is (and is not) monumental rather than ephemeral. They are above-human scale but oddly anthropomorphic. The image is intensely graphic and simple, but its forms are at the threshold of legibility. The material substrate of the image appears crystalline, indeed 'architectural' and strangely fluid. It as though Zygmunt Bauman's idea of 'liquid modernity' has its apotheosis here – as well as its apparent nadir. We might paraphrase this by saying that Holdsworth inverts the nineteenth-century adage that modernity transforms 'all that is solid' into insubstantiality. Here, 'all that was air' – thought of lazily as merely 'virtual' – has become solid – or is it liquid? Or both? The alarming beauty and perfection of the *Spatial Objects* might, in one reading, allow us to imagine them carved out of crystalline rock or another material associated with density, longevity and immovability. This is, of course, entirely intentional; 'data' is associated with insubstantiality, ephemerality, or mobility – mere 'liquidity' in Bauman's now double-edged image. We now know that digital modernity relies on millions of miles of cables laid under oceans and seas; on endless banks of machines lined up in factories like a new proletariat; and on the hard work of hundreds of thousands of labourers in factories with Victorian working conditions. None of these things are insubstantial, and none 'mobile'.

As Gayatri Chakravorty Spivak has remarked, "Globalization takes place only in capital and data. Everything else is damage control." (Spivak 2011: 1). Holdsworth's *Spatial Objects* are not an image of globalization per se, but exemplary artefacts for a world in which we must begin to imagine the operations of data and capital as 'beyond space', at least in the traditional sense. A new spatial imaginary is required to even begin to understand their operations; Holdsworth allows us to begin that process.

Spatial Objects are, furthermore, objects that offer us wilfully contradictory readings, as I have suggested. The first image they present to us is that an object appears 'trapped' inside the work and behind glossy reflective acrylic – literally encased or entombed. It leads us to imagine they are self-contained, autonomous, of their own making. The *Spatial Objects* appear to be 'autotelic' objects – providing their own logic for their existence. We might even imagine they are objects that have brought themselves into being, showing no marks of manufacture and leaving no trace of the means by which they were produced.

It is only upon a closer examination that we 'see past' the reflections to attend to the work as a photograph with an illusionary space behind the picture plane that we look 'into'. At that point we are able to attend to both the sculptural qualities of what is represented 'inside' the picture and to the work's three-dimensional objecthood. The work is both sculpture and photograph, image and object, virtual space and physical reality, it demands that we overcome our existing category divisions and these pairs or polarities become problems, rather than accepted facts, in the works.

One particularly alarming set of implications that *Spatial Objects* offers is that digital technology is akin to a surrogate religion for the twenty-first century. The works' perfection suggests magical containers or talismanic entities possessed of an otherworldly power. If we are offered a God's eye view of a pixel, and by implication of ourselves as a mere GPS location seen from the heavenly position of a satellite, then this reading is redoubled. The objects play with the reflection and refraction of light. The lustrous, clinical, alluring perfection of their surface attracts us whilst deferring, preventing them becoming objects of knowledge. As objects, the works are both equally resistant to being internalised by any empathetic gaze, and to being internalised intellectually. There is no means for *Spatial Objects* to be classified within the ordinary taxonomy of objects we possess; they remain immune to being penetrated, visually or conceptually.

This is in part achieved by their play with depth and

with surface, as well as the kind of gaze they presuppose and allow. One distinction that springs to mind when viewing the objects is the art critic Michael Fried's famous polarity between pictorial works of art that are 'theatrical' and those which are 'absorptive'. 'Theatrical' works project out to the world, as propaganda does; 'absorptive' images, of which a Vermeer would be the ultimate example, lure us into an illusionary space within or beyond the picture plane. Which description do we imagine Holdsworth's *Spatial Objects* occupies? Characteristically the works defy being readily classified as either. Instead, they can only be categorised in terms of 'both / and', or 'neither / nor'.

A framework of 'neither / nor' is, perhaps, another ideal way to view the works. As Holdsworth notes, they intentionally resemble Minimalist artworks in the tradition created by figures such as Donald Judd, and John McCracken. McCracken's redirection of empty minimalist 'form' with unexpected 'content' is especially appropriate here. It is effectively impossible to project ourselves into or attribute any obvious state of affect onto *Spatial Objects*. Their lack of narrative, distance from existing forms of representation, and avoidance of clear points of interpretive reference renders them resistant to description or a sense of identification. As I have remarked, they cannot be easily described adjectivally; indeed they might be described as being resistant to any incorporation into language. They assert the oddity and inexplicability of their materiality in the way that Judd's best works do.

They occupy the anomalous position of both 'aesthetic' objects (concepts made sensible and inspiring states of affect) and being akin to canonical works of conceptual art in that their 'true' content can be identified as a philosophical speculation upon our knowledge of the world as well as the media of representation we have to frame it by.

If the works offer us a three-dimensional image of 'perfection' – seemingly untouched by human hand – this is heightened, literally and metaphorically, by the fact that they seem to be gently floating off the ground or suspended in mid-air. The larger works in the series offer a small but discernible shadow gap between themselves and the gallery floor that gives the impression they are weightless, as well as timeless and oddly, formless. They appear both to levitate and to be irredeemably earth-bound. In this, the objects seem to offer figures of both gravity and grace. Their elegance and crystalline clarity of form suggest diamond-like qualities – as if they were hard and impenetrable and each had been brought into being or sent back to our present from an impossible future by some force beyond our imagination.

In this they also evoke both a peculiar form of sublimity and a strange self-containment. One of the classical criteria for assessing sublimity in its earliest formulations was 'formlessness' but this could scarcely be less applicable here, especially in terms of the object as sculpture. And yet it could scarcely be more apposite in terms of the object-as-image, the pixel represented. The shapes of the pixels inside the object always exceed the boundaries of the frame, so that we are aware of their seemingly limitless energy and their potential.

On the one hand, the shape – the image offered to mind by Holdsworth's *Spatial Objects* is readily identifiable, even nameable. They are all created as almost perfect geometric figures. Crucially, they are pyramidal, rather than seen as two-dimensional rectangular windows, so that they occupy a peculiar position between photographic picture plane, digital screen, and sculptural volume possessed of considerable mass and weight. Each object is also almost anthropomorphic in scale, standing above human height.

The sharply tapering pyramidal forms also suggest that the objects are sentries or sentinels confronting us, having arrived from another realm. Confronting the objects in space – rather than viewing them in reproduction – one can be filled with the alarming sense that the objects are looking at us, rather than us at them. We cannot penetrate or interrogate. This is, of course, a result of having to slide between registers of 'seeing in' and 'seeing as', as philosopher Richard Wollheim's has described it. We are offered an illusion of 'virtual' space and then denied it; then we encounter a 'real' object in three-dimensional space. The forms are fields of glowing light and colour that draw our eyes into them as well as geometric sculptures. Their scale and their dimensions are two different things.

This peculiar kind of sublimity, in which the smallest of objects has the greatest of claims to power, is a uniquely modern one. Edmund Burke's theories of the sublime, in the mid-eighteenth century, mostly focussed upon an image of nature larger than human scale, and more powerful than human agency could conceive of, or counter.

As we have seen, Holdsworth's works to date have often remodelled and remade this pre-existing concept for an age in which the very idea of 'nature' has become problematized (by figures such as Bruno Latour, most notably, a philosopher who Holdsworth much admires). Latour's speculative investigations into the lives of objects has provided a theoretically grounded set of investigations that parallel the science fiction parables of writers such as J.G. Ballard, who imagined objects as developing their own agency, sentience, or energy-fields. Latour's canonical work provides one lens through which to view *Spatial Objects* and their apparent agency. Their machine-like, technological aesthetic and 'finish-fetish' (to use a term from post-minimalist art), recall the heyday of science fiction in which machines gained sentience of their own and began to look for a stake in the world equal to or greater than our own. However, I propose that only a threefold reading of the kinds of sublimity on offer in *Spatial Objects* is adequate to a complexity that draws together Holdsworth's scientific, spatial-geographical and medial-representational interests. We might say that these are the atomic, technological, and temporal sublimes.

Firstly, in their self-containment, lambency or

luminosity, and with their sense that they are radiating light from within, *Spatial Objects* appear to be all but radioactive. Their 'inner light' seems to emanate its own distinctive frequencies, as though the objects had wavelengths particular to themselves. They seem to be living out an atomic half-life, possessing a barely contained and latent energy. This reading suggests the works as miniature suns, stars illuminating their own universe. It is no accident that the objects are displayed spotlit, as though light emanates from them to us, and human subjects are decentred from the universe. Their unnervingly, intensely saturated colour-fields recall the image of a vast universe crackling with energy (as envisaged by Colour Field painters like Barnett Newman.) The imaginative implication is that a single object contains an immensity of energy – that a pixel is much like an atom in its power, its possibilities, even its destructive potential; as firmly placed in its position as the microcosmic building block of the virtual world as the atom is in the real.

As I have suggested, digital imaging is, today, effectively the sole means we have to see and interpret the world beyond our immediate experience. All our visual experience is now mediated through the prior representation of the world in pixels. Pixels are the visual building blocks by which the world can be known. Prior to Holdsworth, few artists have stopped to consider the philosophical or technological bases of what a pixel is. We scarcely ever 'see' a pixel per se, despite our reliance upon them for the creation and dissemination of every form of knowledge. Holdsworth opens up the range of figures and metaphors by which the digital world can be thought of and imagined.

Secondly, in *Spatial Objects*, Holdsworth's evocation of a technological sublime is achieved through several means. He ensures that we only ever encounter one individual plane of a pixel seen as a free-floating and three-dimensional entity. In the artist's own words, what we are made witness to is a 'fragment of a fragment'. As outlined, the work 'distils' his previous work into its smallest constituent element – the single pixel in digital space. Ordinarily such an object is literally microscopic, but as I have suggested above, there is a structural link not only between the microscopic and microcosmic, but the microscopic and the macrocosmic. Might we, then, continue to imagine Holdsworth as a twenty-first century Romantic and the heir to William Blake's desire "to see the world in a grain of sand" – allowing us to view the universe within a fragment of a pixel?

We should, then, also see *Spatial Objects* as embodying a thoroughly Blakean but nonetheless twenty-first century technological or 'post-human' sublime, especially via the work of the critic and historian David Nye (1994) and the cultural theorist Jeremy Gilbert-Rolfe (1999) respectively. As the latter remarks, "The limitlessness once found in nature gives way, in technology, to a limitlessness produced out of an idea which is not interested in being an idea of nature, but one which *replaces* the idea of nature" (my italics). Gilbert-Rolfe observes that in the Oxford English Dictionary, this 'traditional' sublime presents an image of "grandeur, or beauty as to inspire great admiration or awe": Holdsworth's *Spatial Objects* invite all of these readings. They inspire 'awe' in recalling the famous Monolith from Stanley Kubrick's epic 2001: A Space Odyssey (1968). Kubrick authorised that the object's name should be capitalised as a proper noun, as though it was a sentient being. Such a line of imaginative enquiry prompts the thought that pixels are our modern-day 'monoliths' in that they have ignited life on earth; that pixels live through us, and that they are also our creators, and we mere parasites or proxies. Indeed many of the most likely interpretations of *Spatial Objects* suggest an inversion of the 'virtual' and the 'real' worlds wherein our familiar physical world has become 'virtualised' and the digital realm made palpable, even threatening or predatorial in its physicality.

Thirdly, if *Spatial Objects* evoke the images of the future through the fiction and science fiction of the twentieth century, they also play with our sense of time in more alarming ways. They offer a temporal sublime. Being sealed under acrylic, as if entombed, the Objects appear to be inaccessible and as relics or ruins from another era, marooned in a perpetual present. As the philosopher Edmond Couchot has written, the digital realm is treated in a cavalier fashion that no other medium would suffer: "The preservation of the digital arts, and more generally of the digital culture, raises one of the most complex issues that human societies have had to solve in their relation with history." (Couchot 2013 n.p.)

We might, then, be better served viewing Holdsworth's works not only as sentinels sent back to us from the future, but also as vessels launched into the future as time-capsules. We might view them as vital records of what the mineral technologies of the early twenty-first century made possible – momentarily – before the scale and rapacity of extraction that made them possible swiftly made them technologically 'extinct'. In scarcely a generation or two, the tantalum, tungsten and gold that are used to manufacture our mobile phones will be fully extracted. It has, as yet, struck very few people that we are reaching 'peak pixel'. Holdsworth suggests that our own age sits between an endless pre-digital vista on one side, and a post-digital world on the other. He also suggests that this time inside the digital realm has – for the moment – transformed our imaginative relation to time itself. Couchot suggests that the virtual realm exists in a kind of 'u-chronia': a utopia of time rather than space (ibid). This time-space is both entirely historically specific, and experienced as if floating free of historical determinants and material manufacture. *Spatial Objects* are both u-chronic objects, and memento mori for the age of extraction.

If this reading is convincing, then we may remember that throughout his career, Holdsworth's work has taken the form of an investigation into the ontology of the photographic image in the twenty-first century as the principal way in which time is 'captured' and known. *Spatial Objects* presents us with what he has labelled the "surface interface of the image". Holdsworth suggests that we might have a sublimity of surface. A half-generation ago, Alicia Imperiale argued in her volume New Flatness that issues about 'surface' associated with "the aesthetics of the computer screen" had a special currency in art and architecture. This was because "in its very nature a surface is an unstable condition: for where are its boundaries? What is its status?" (Imperiale 2000: 1). These words continue to be applicable in describing *Spatial Objects* – but the assumptions they rest on have been reversed.

Holdsworth inverts Imperiale's equation between structure and surface. He describes his concerns as with "the architecture of the virtual" (rather than virtualising architecture). Here, we get to grips with the structure of the digital, rather than the virtualisation of structure. We might best describe an encounter with *Spatial Objects* as seeing the world from a pixel's point of view: as though we had been transposed onto the other side of a computer screen and were looking outwards to the 'real' world of human subjectivity. In Holdsworth's own words the works function as an "interface between the 'real lived breathed' and the 'digital lived breathed'". In his imagination, the virtual realm must be taken as an equally important space to that 'outside' of the screen; the two are inseparable and equally valid domains. As he remarks, "new thinking about scale" has been fundamental to the development of the work; the objects should also be read as "interfaces between the surfacing dimensions of the dimensions of the [entire] earth, and the dimensions of the digital, when visualising a single point of data." The term 'interface' is crucial here; the work is an imaginative 'interface' between thinking upon the macro scale of planetary, globalization data processes and mapping, and the micro scale of binary information as code.

Once 'inside' the virtual realm, space operates in a different fashion: scale does indeed need to be thought of differently, and there are many such thinkers who have risen to this challenge in the digital humanities, across disciplines from geography to anthropology. The less obvious but more important observation here must be that there is no conception of space that does not have a correlating conception of time to validate it. In *Spatial Objects*, time operates in a wholly different way to that determined by human metabolisms, and the diurnal rhythms set by the sun.

These are not Wordsworthian landscapes of wholesome plenitude and permanence. They are unmapped, unknown spaces: indeed the only unmapped spaces remaining to us.

This, I propose, is where the title *Spatial Objects* becomes wilfully misleading. These are best seen as temporal objects – but objects of special complexity and contradiction. They appear out-of-time. These are, at the same time 'u-chronic' objects and deeply historical ones, time capsules of the early twenty-first century. Or, as Melanie Vandenbrouck has observed, these works "occupy liminal spaces, at the confluence of art and science; the analogue and digital; macro and micro; the empirical and the philosophical." (Vandenbrouck 2015 n.p.)

Augé, M., (1995) Non-places: Introduction to an Anthropology of Supermodernity, London: Verso

Couchot, E., (2013) 'History Time and "Uchronic" Time: Another Perspective on Memory and Oblivion', paper at The Digital Oblivion, Zentrum für Kunst und Medientechnologie (ZKM), Karlsruhe, [online] posted 2013, accessed 21 April 2016, available at http://www.hybrid.univ-paris8.fr/lodel/index.php?id=215

Craven, T., (2015) Gilbert-Rolfe, J., (1999) Beauty and the Contemporary Sublime, New York: Allworth Press

Imperiale, A., (2000), New Flatness: Surface Tension in Digital Architecture, Basel: Birkäuser

Lefebvre, H., (1991), The Production of Space, Oxford: Wiley-Blackwell

Nye, D.E., (1994), American Technological Sublime, Camb MA: MIT Press

Spivak, G.C., (2011), An Aesthetic Education in the Era of Globalization, Camb MA: Harvard University Press

Vandenbrouck, M., (2015) 'Dan Holdsworth's dizzyingly beautiful photographs on show in Southampton', Apollo magazine, [online] posted 11 June 2015, accessed 1 March 2016, available at http://www.apollo-magazine.com/dan-holdsworths-dizzyingly-beautiful-photographs-on-show-in-southampton/

No.36

No.51

No.161

No.38

No.166

No.17

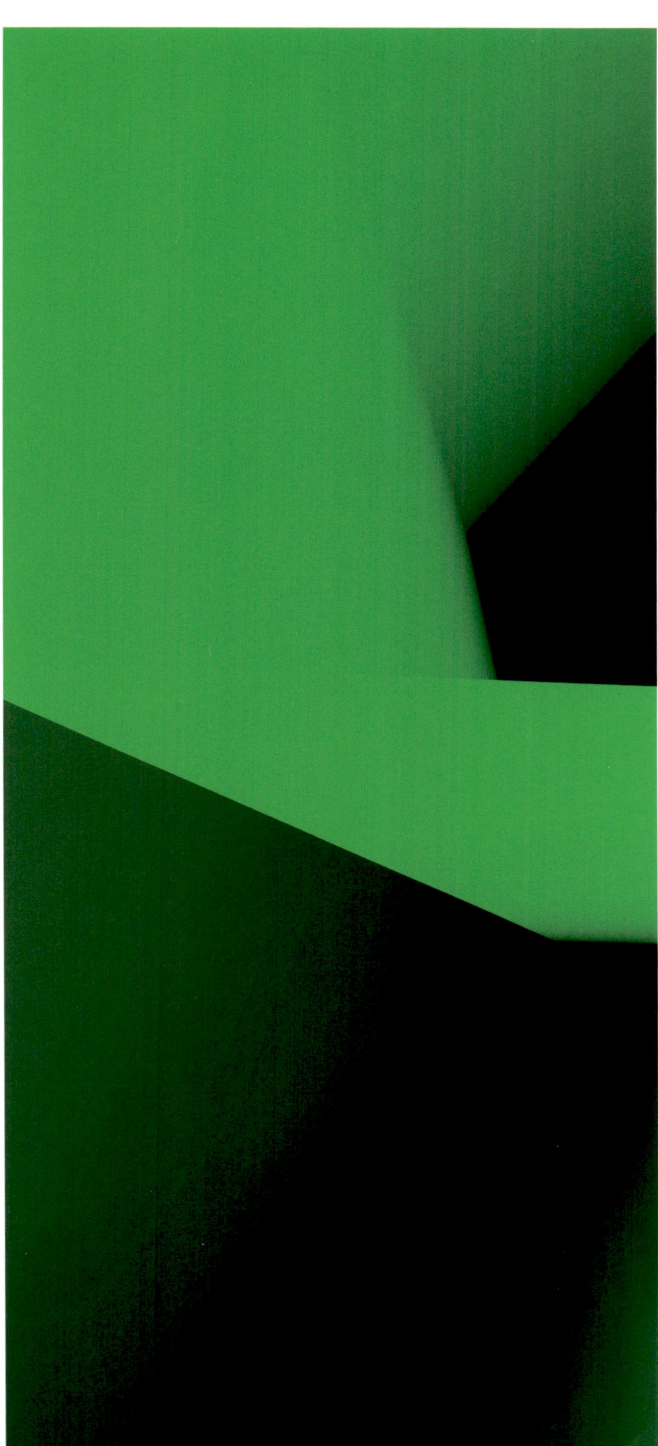

No.259

No.154

No.40

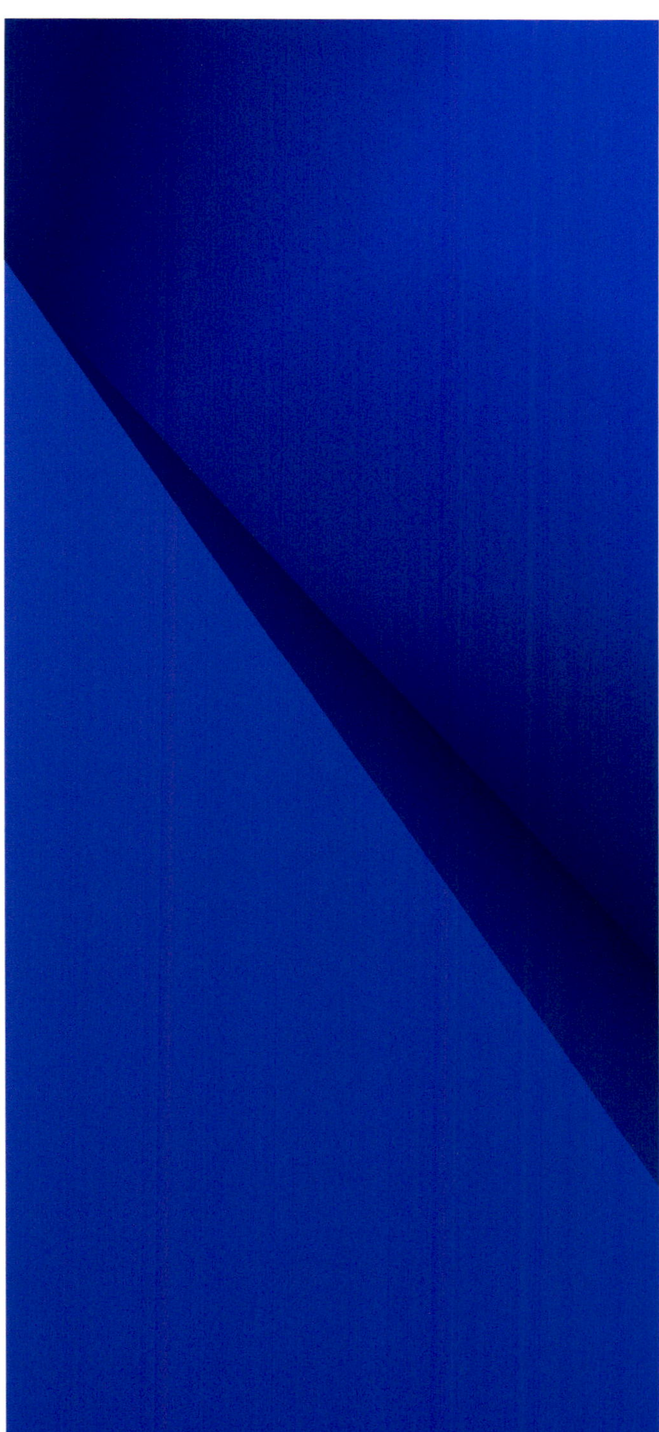

No.105

No.180

No.163

No.164

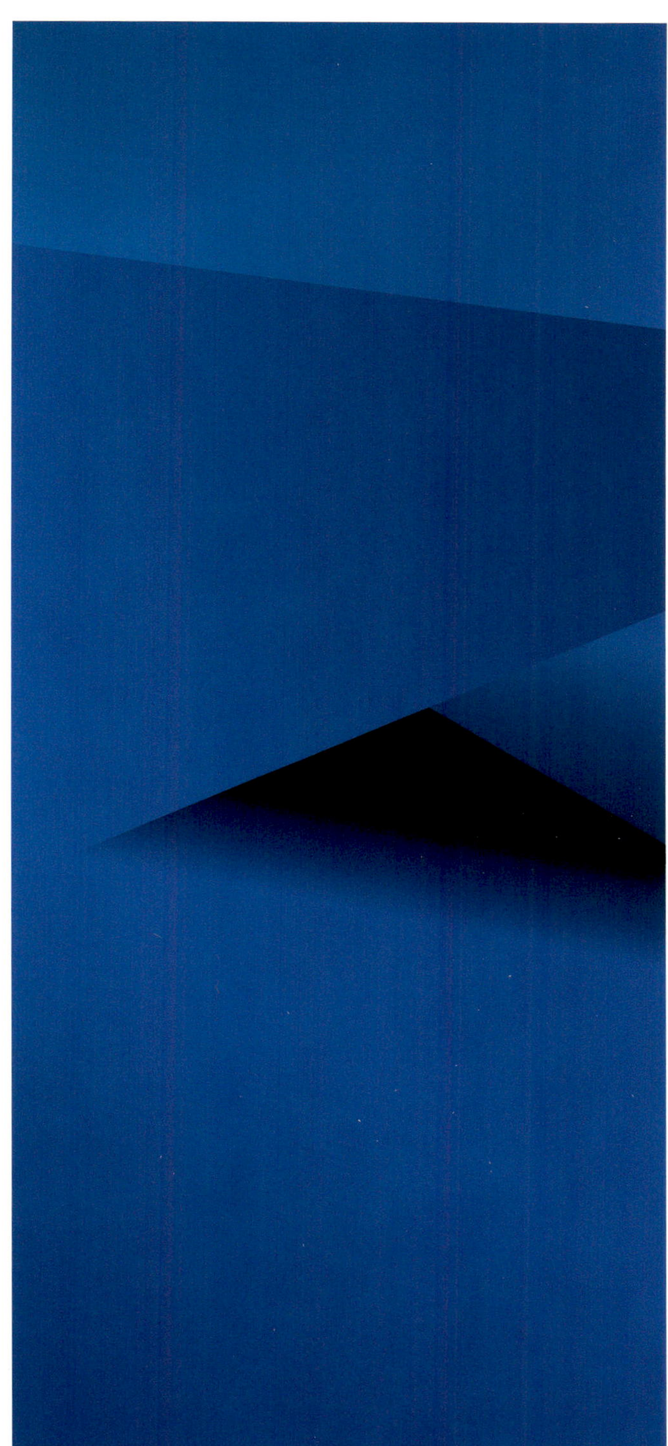

No.08

No.201

No.248

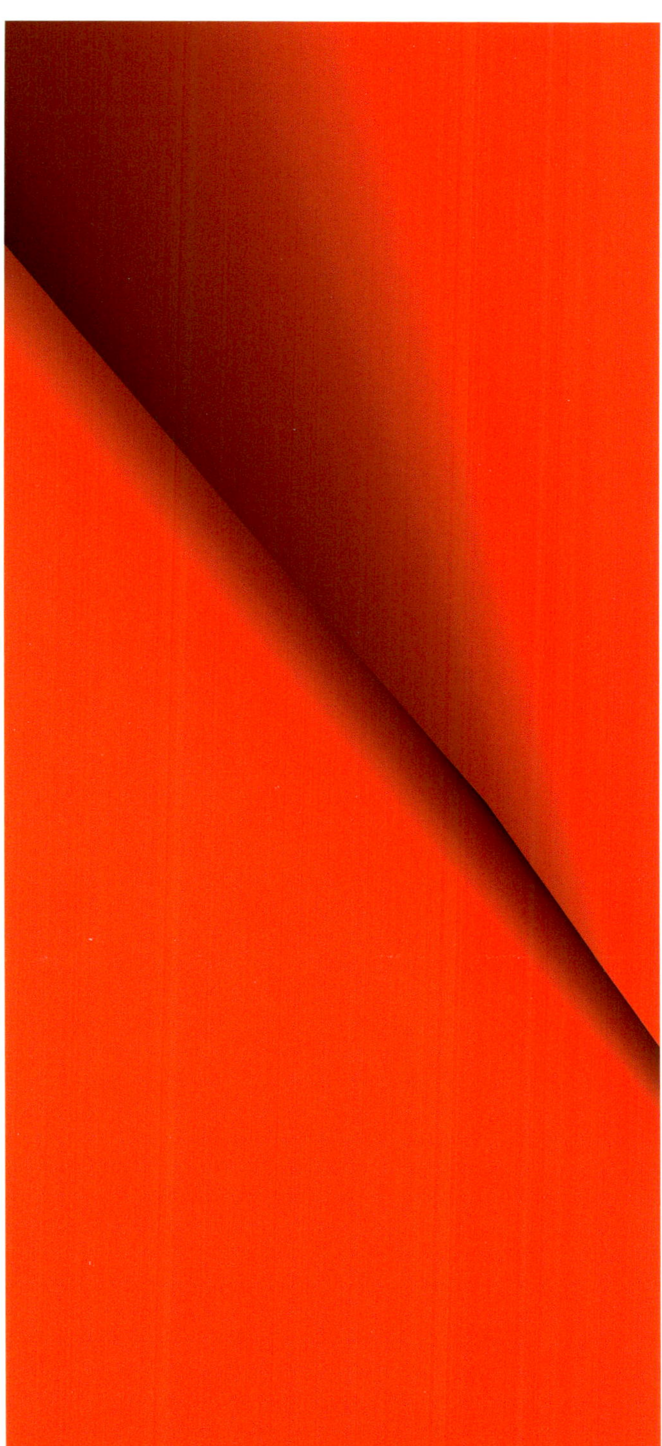

No.184

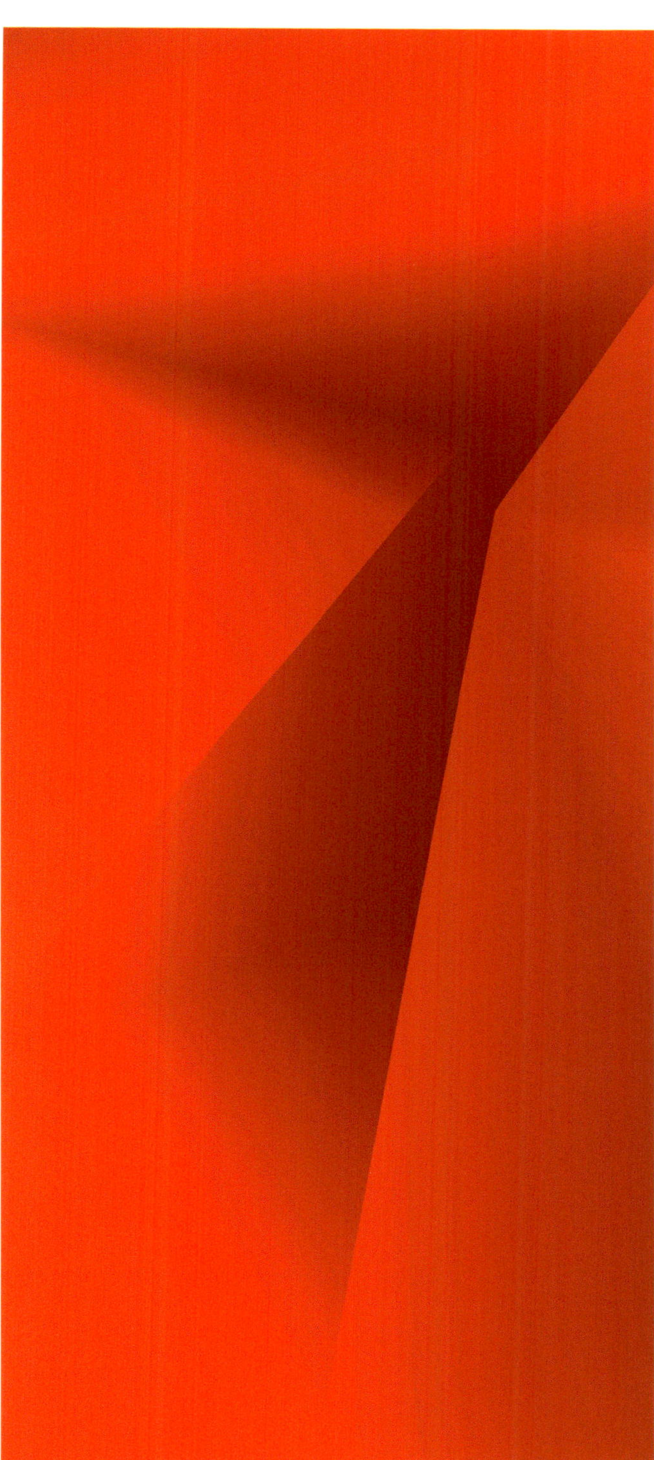

No.143

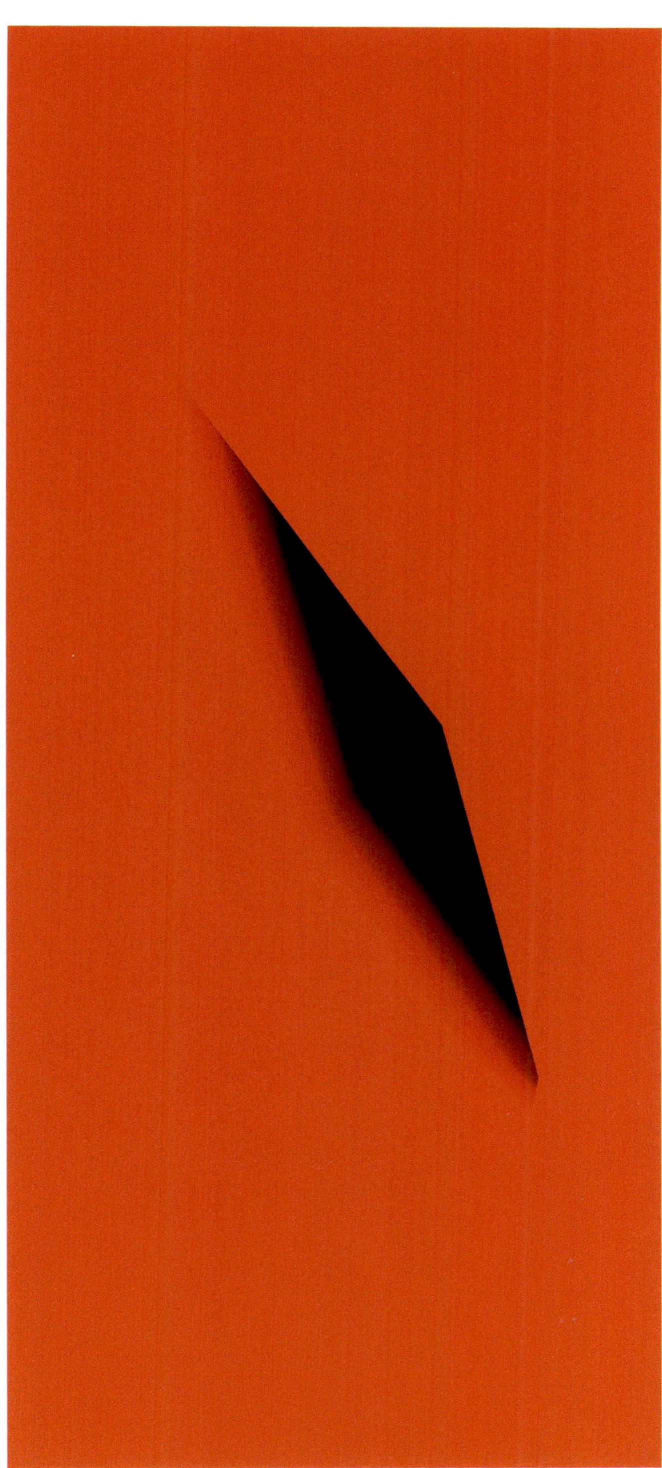

No.131

No.126

No.270

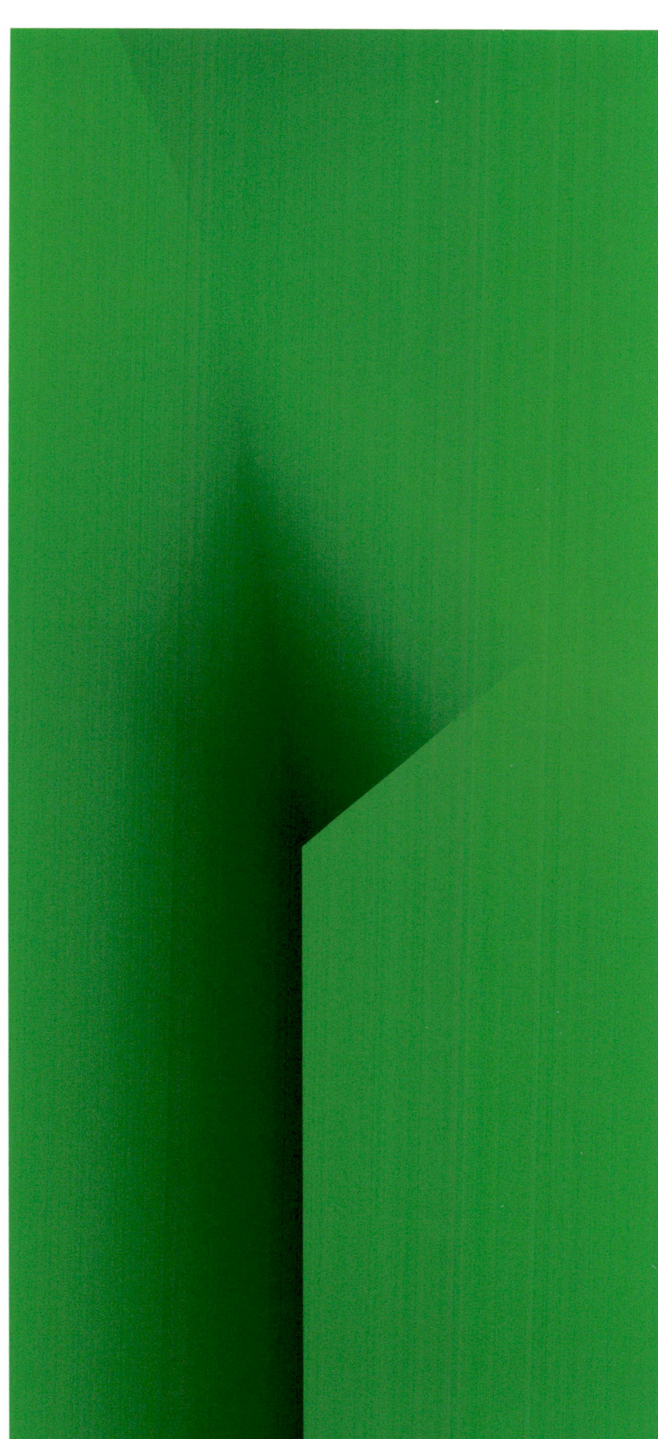

No.279

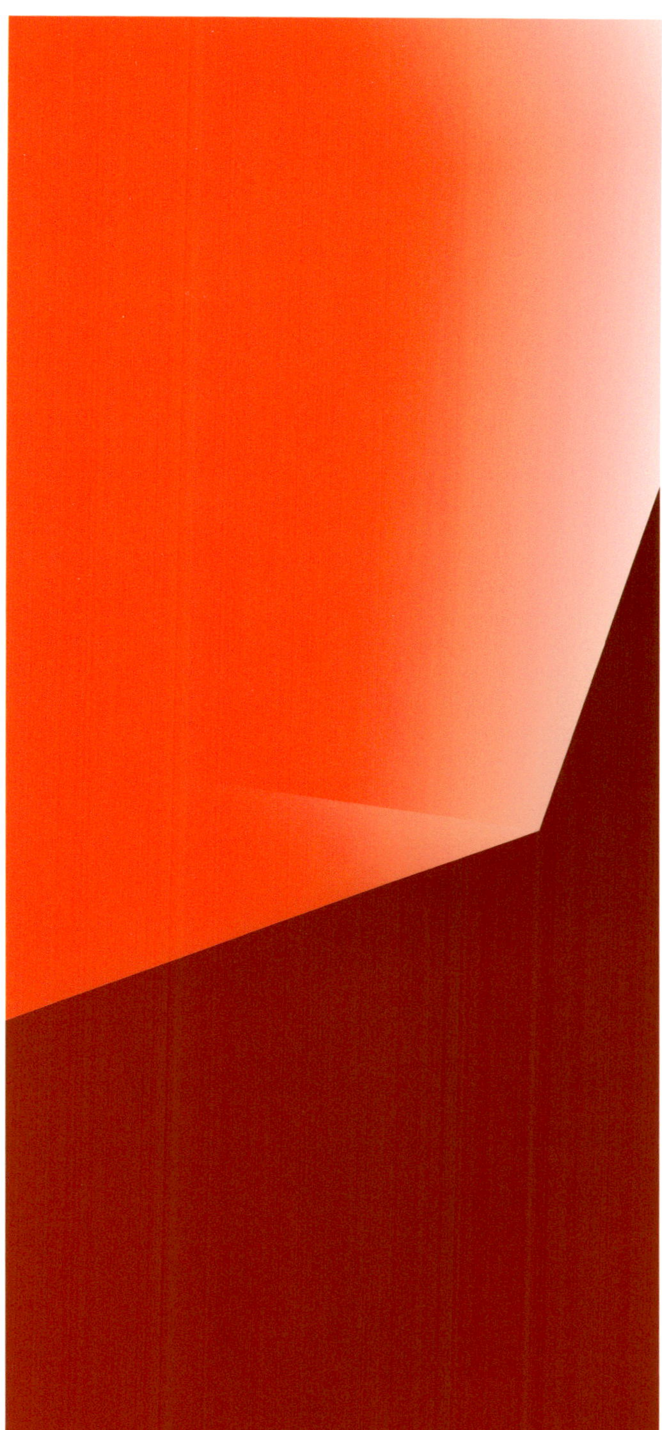

No.250

No.280

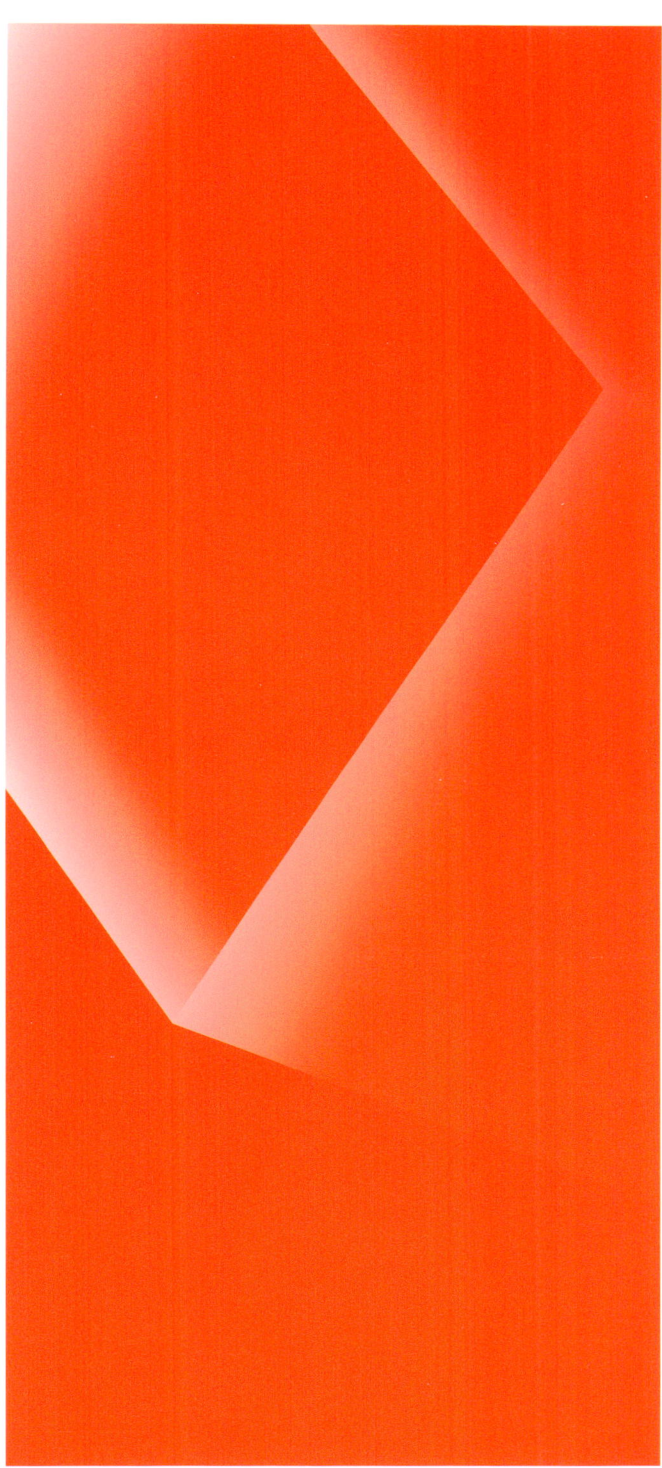

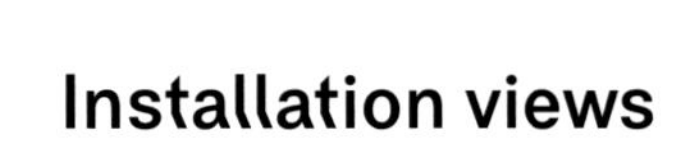

Installation views

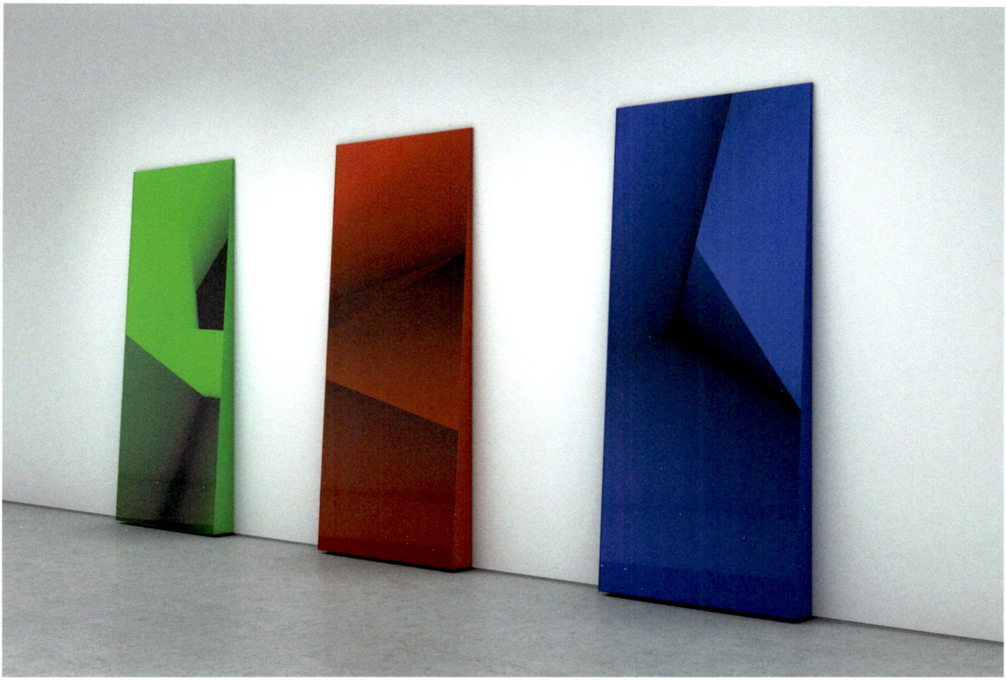

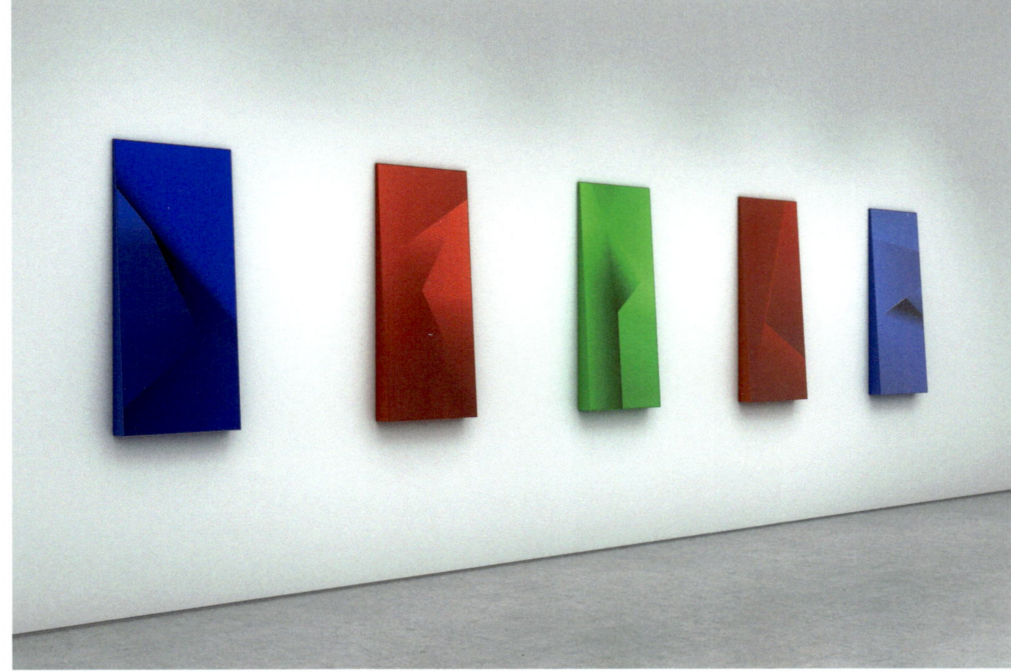

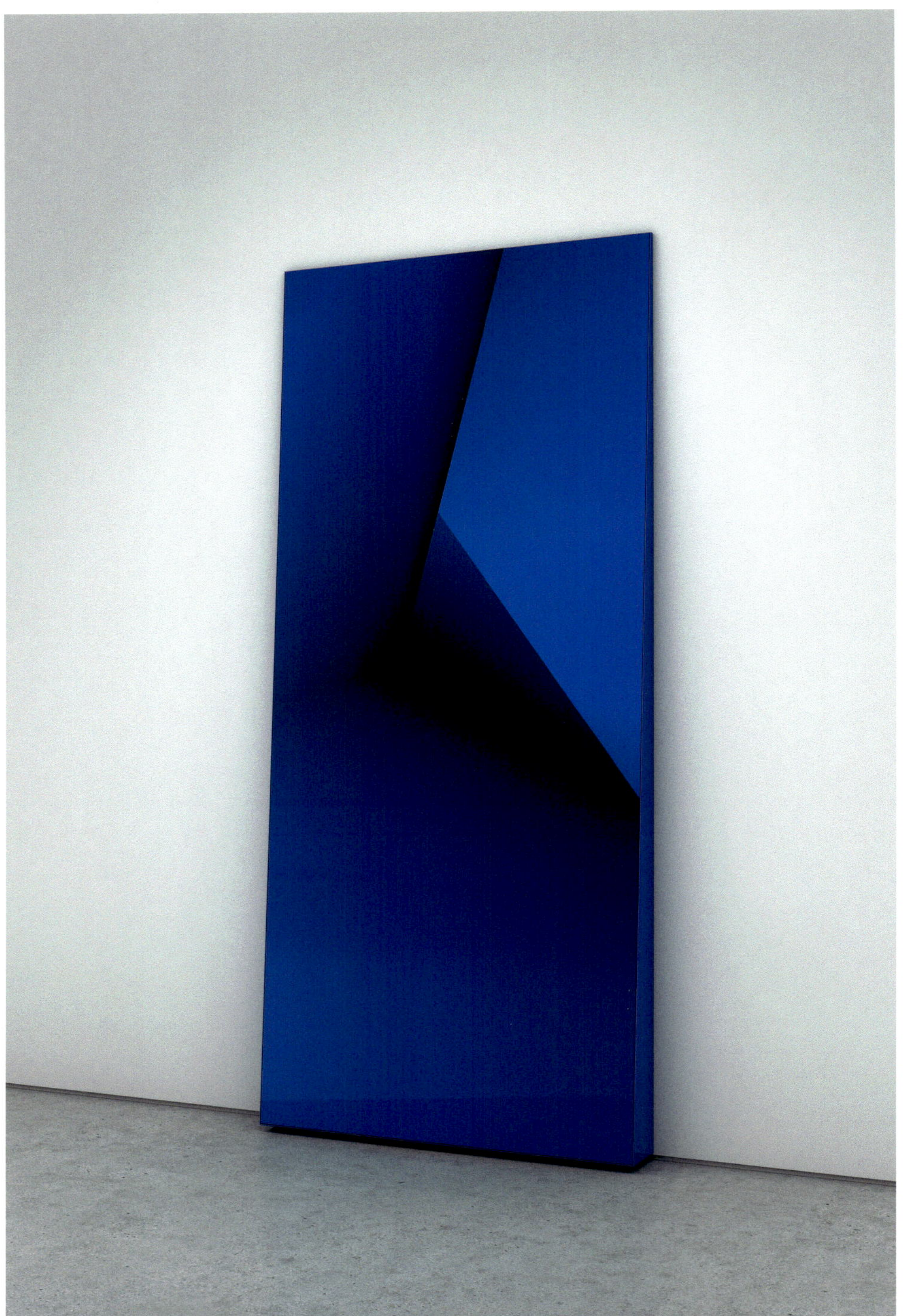

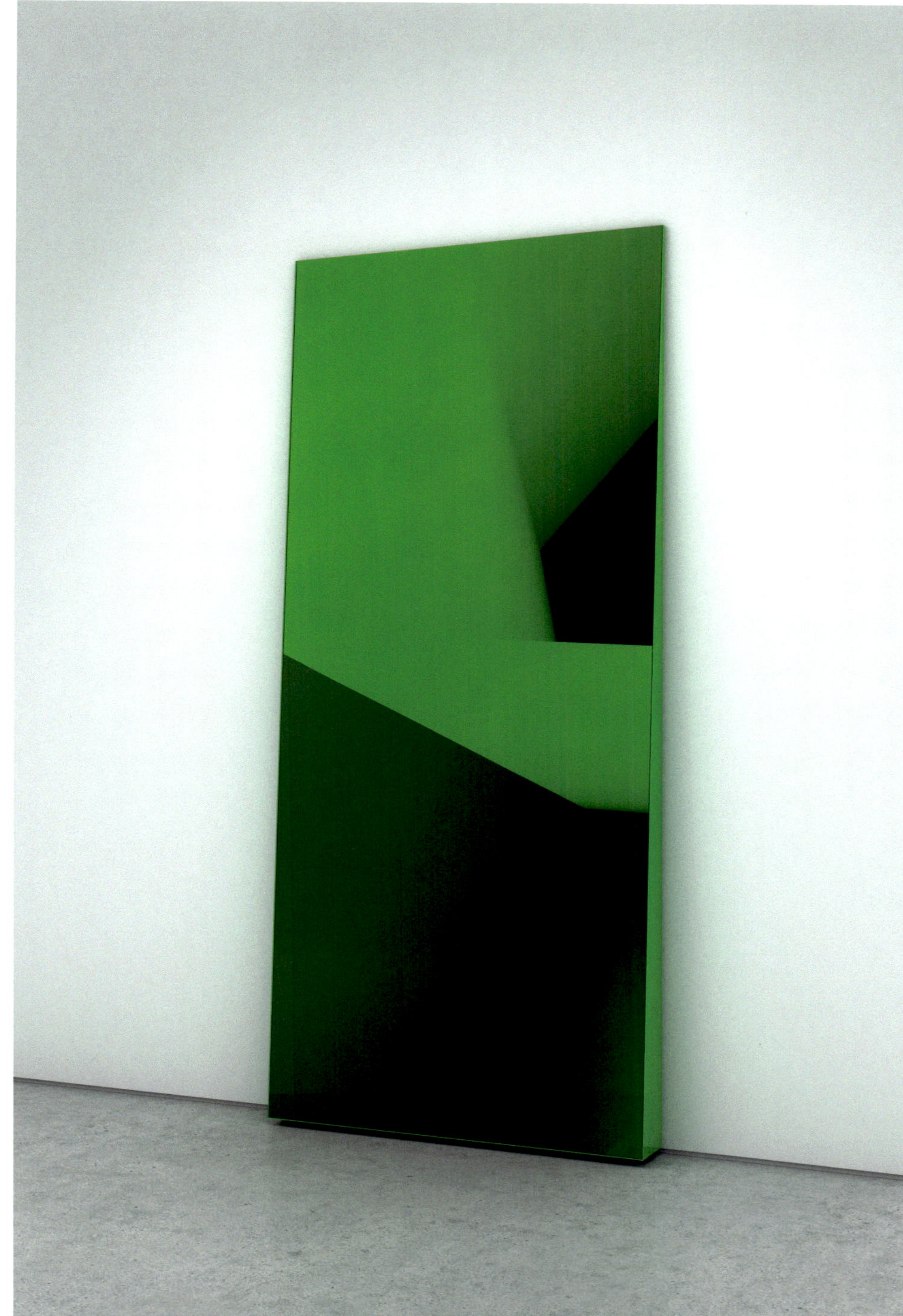

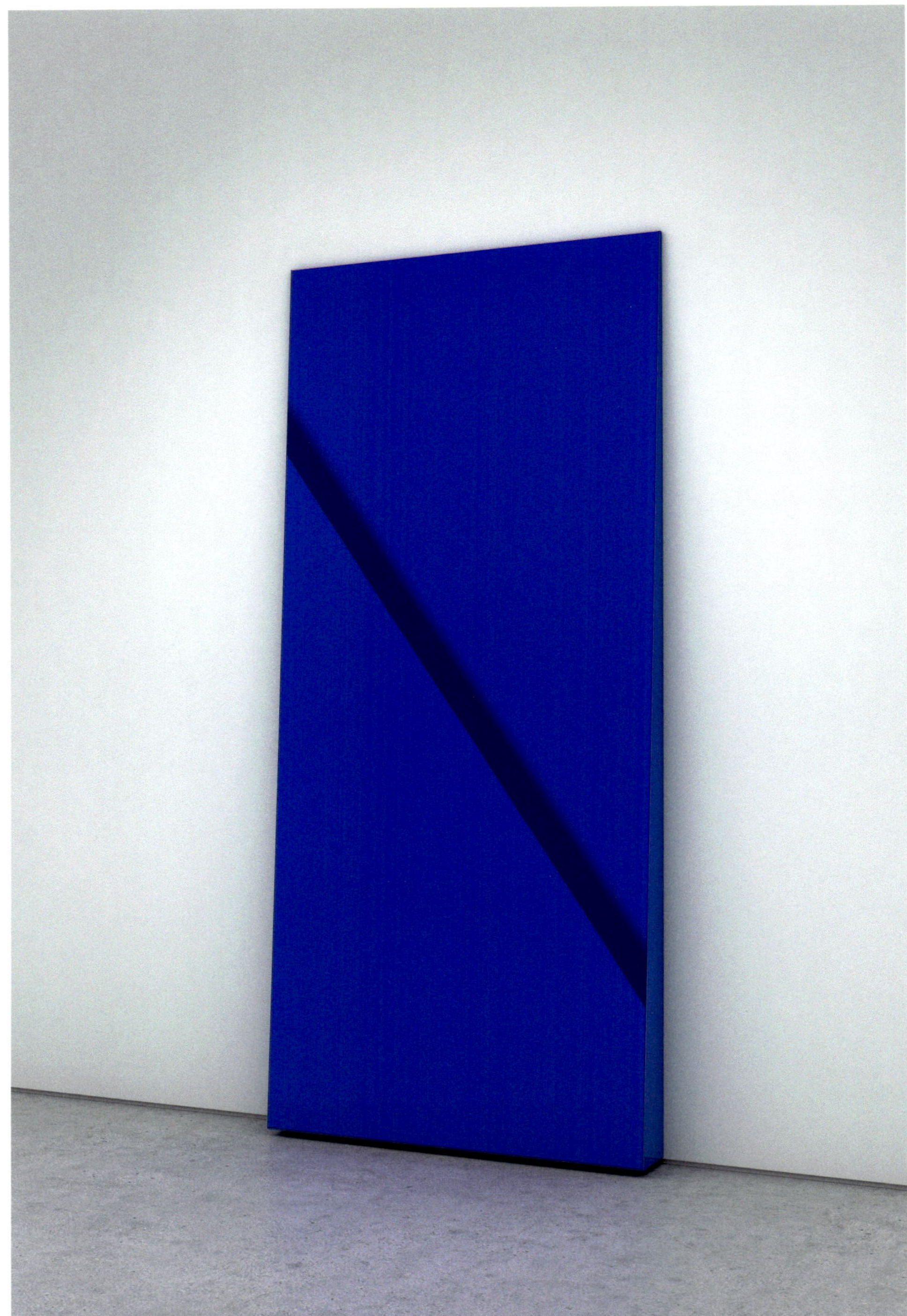

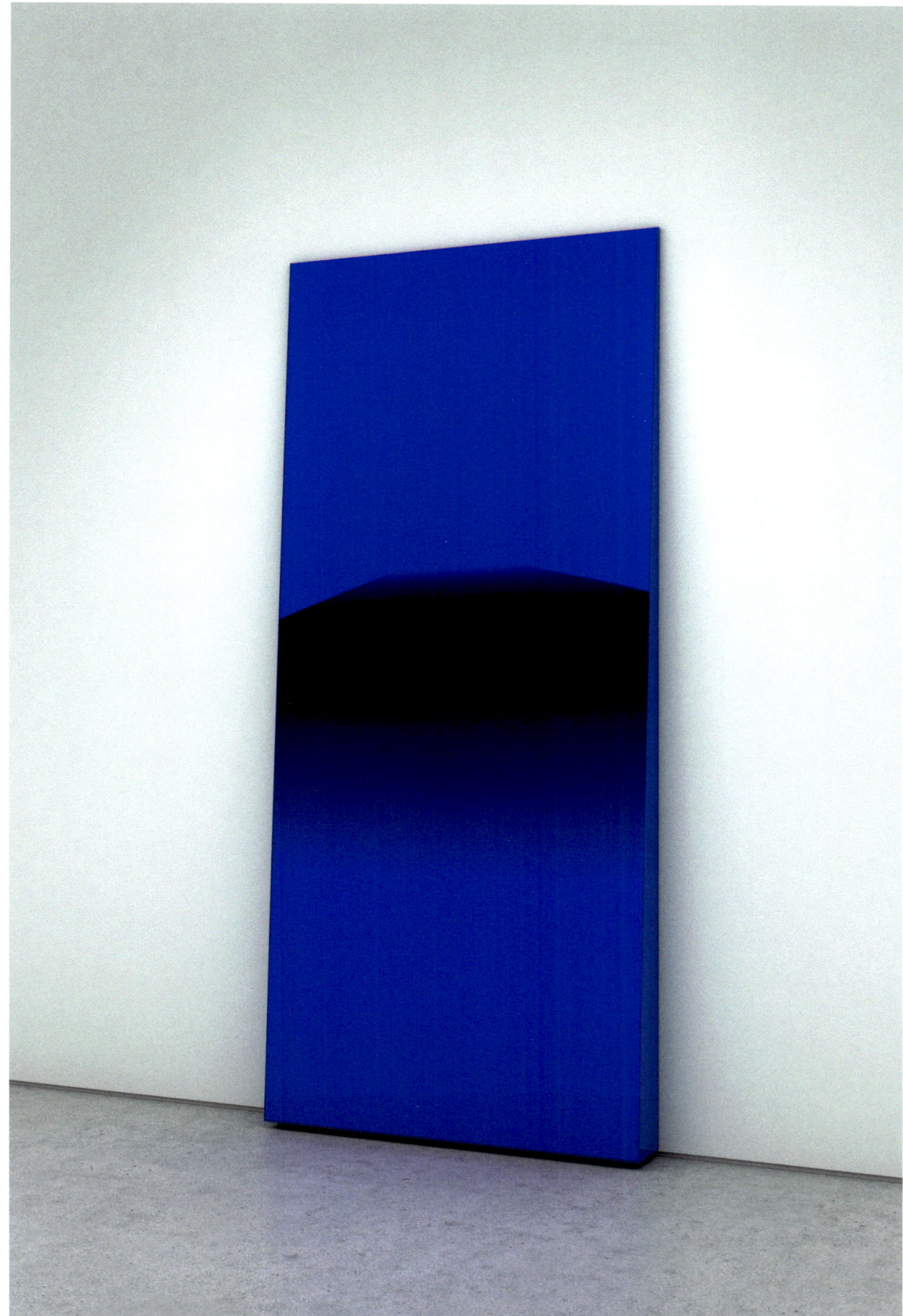

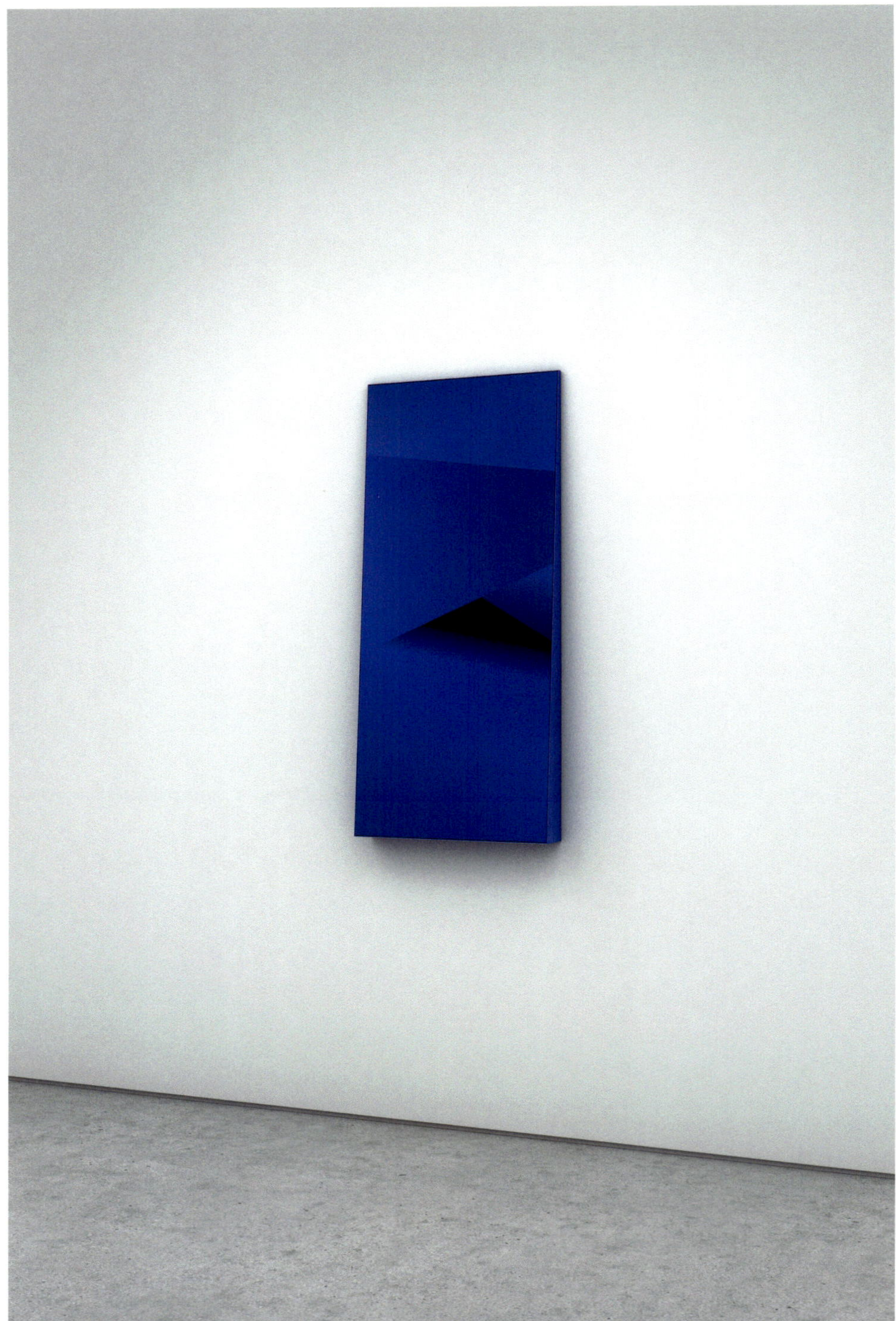

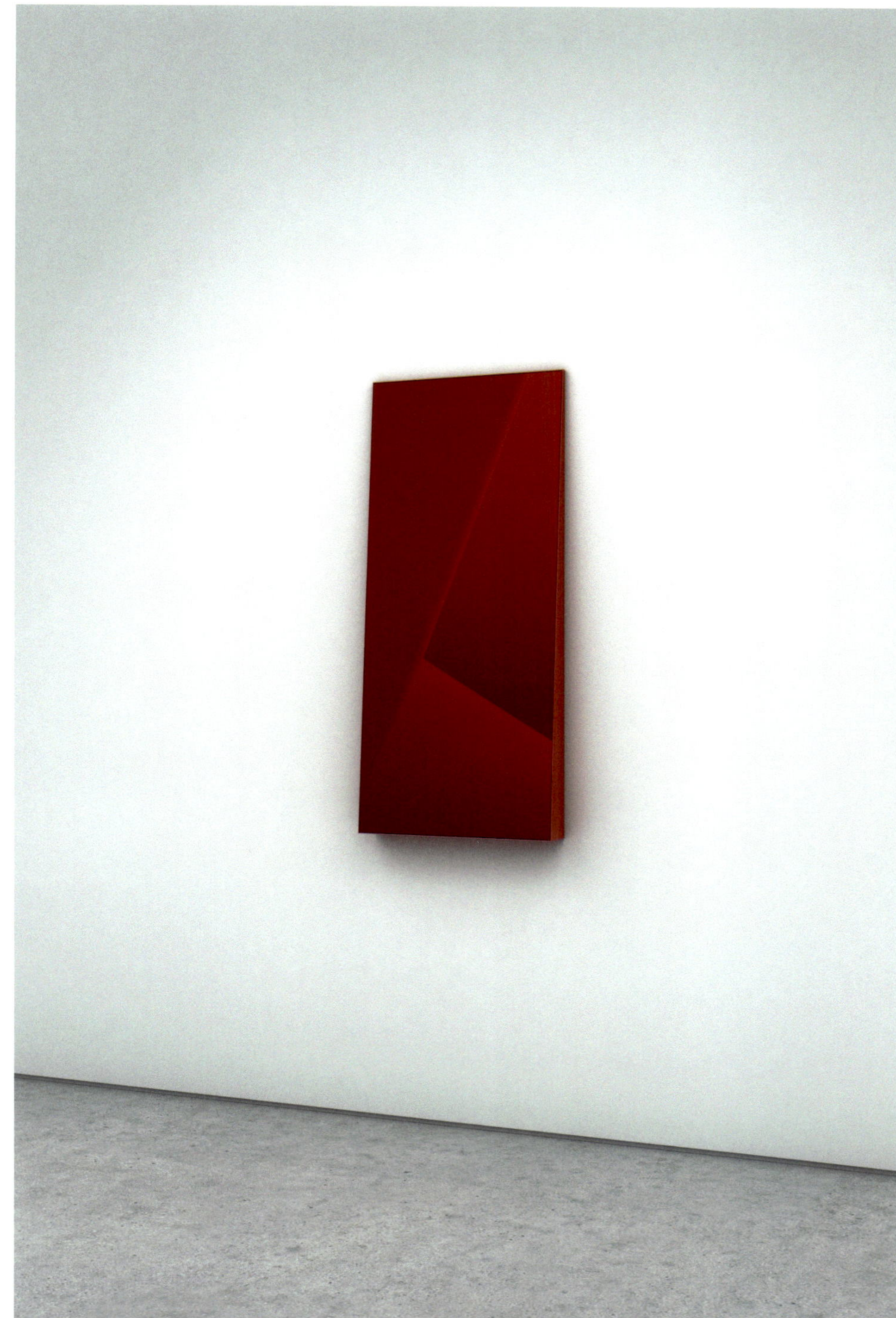

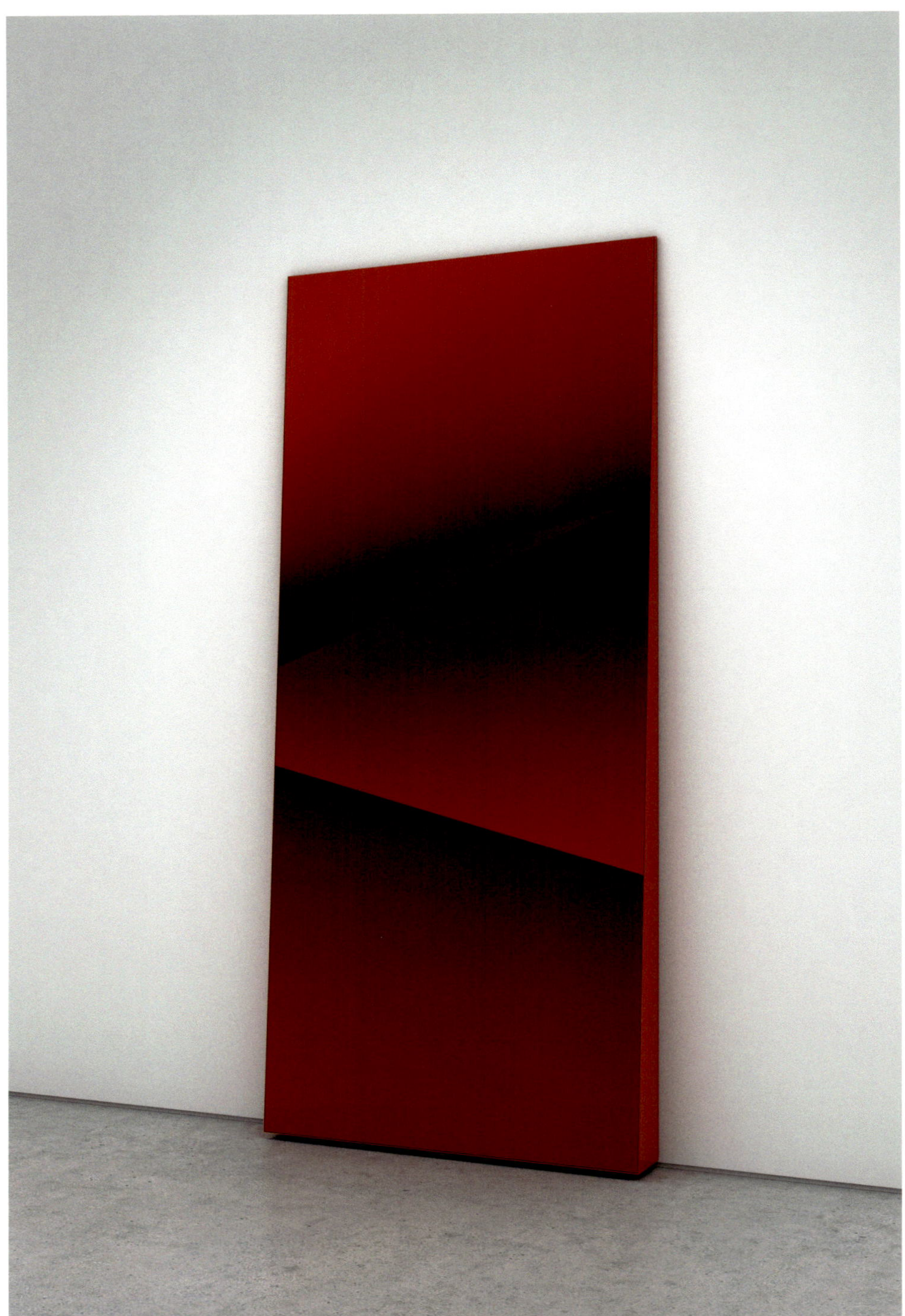

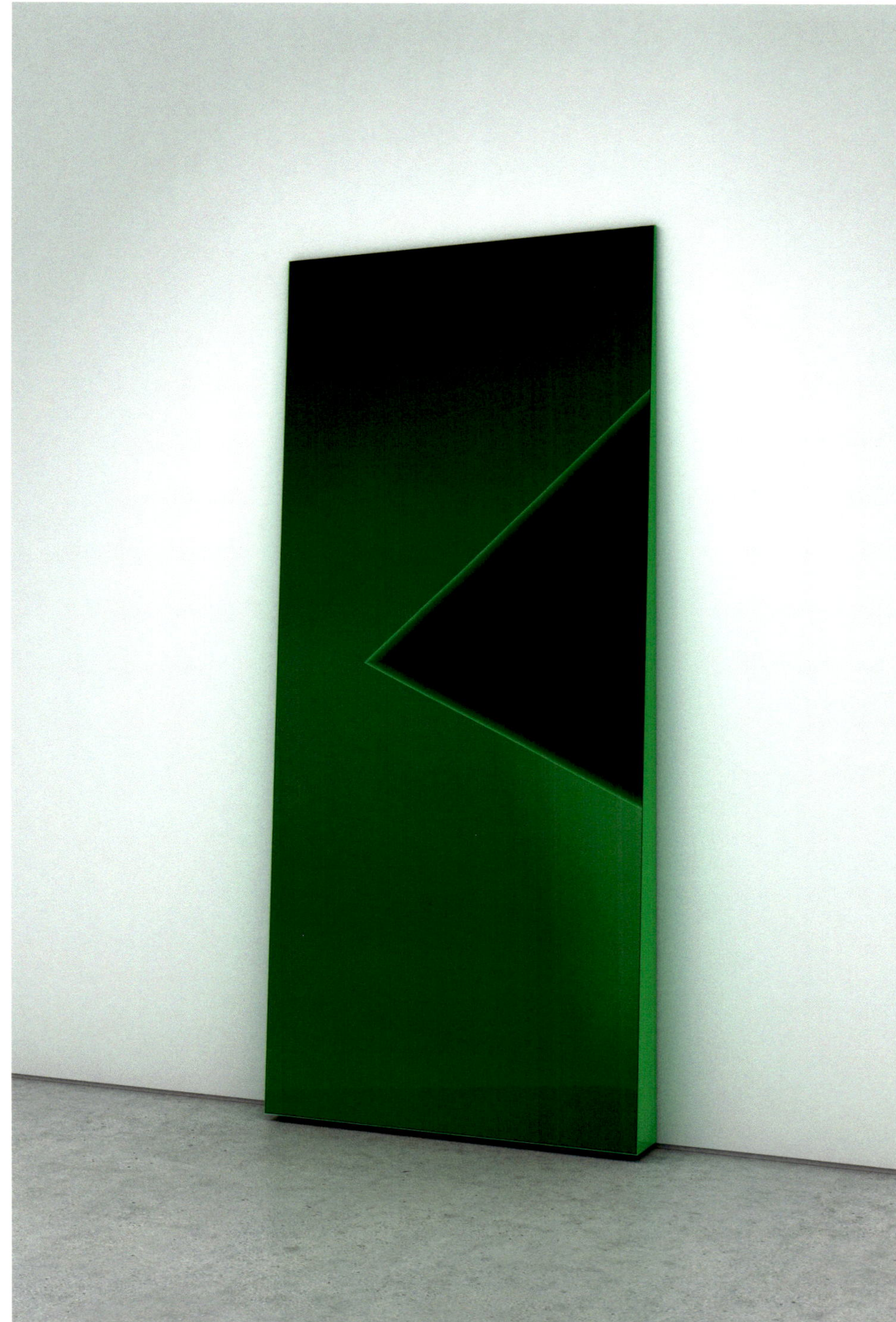

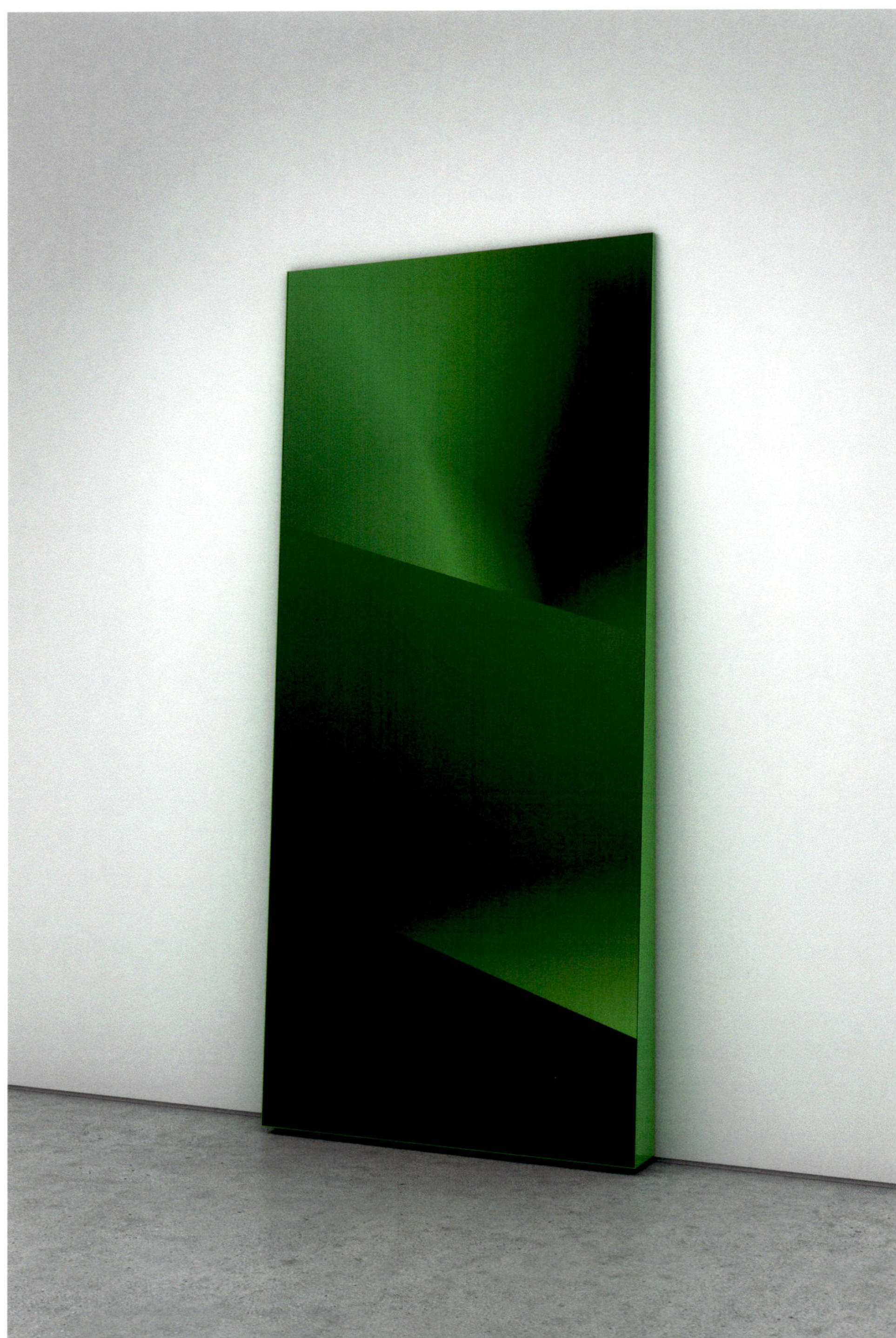

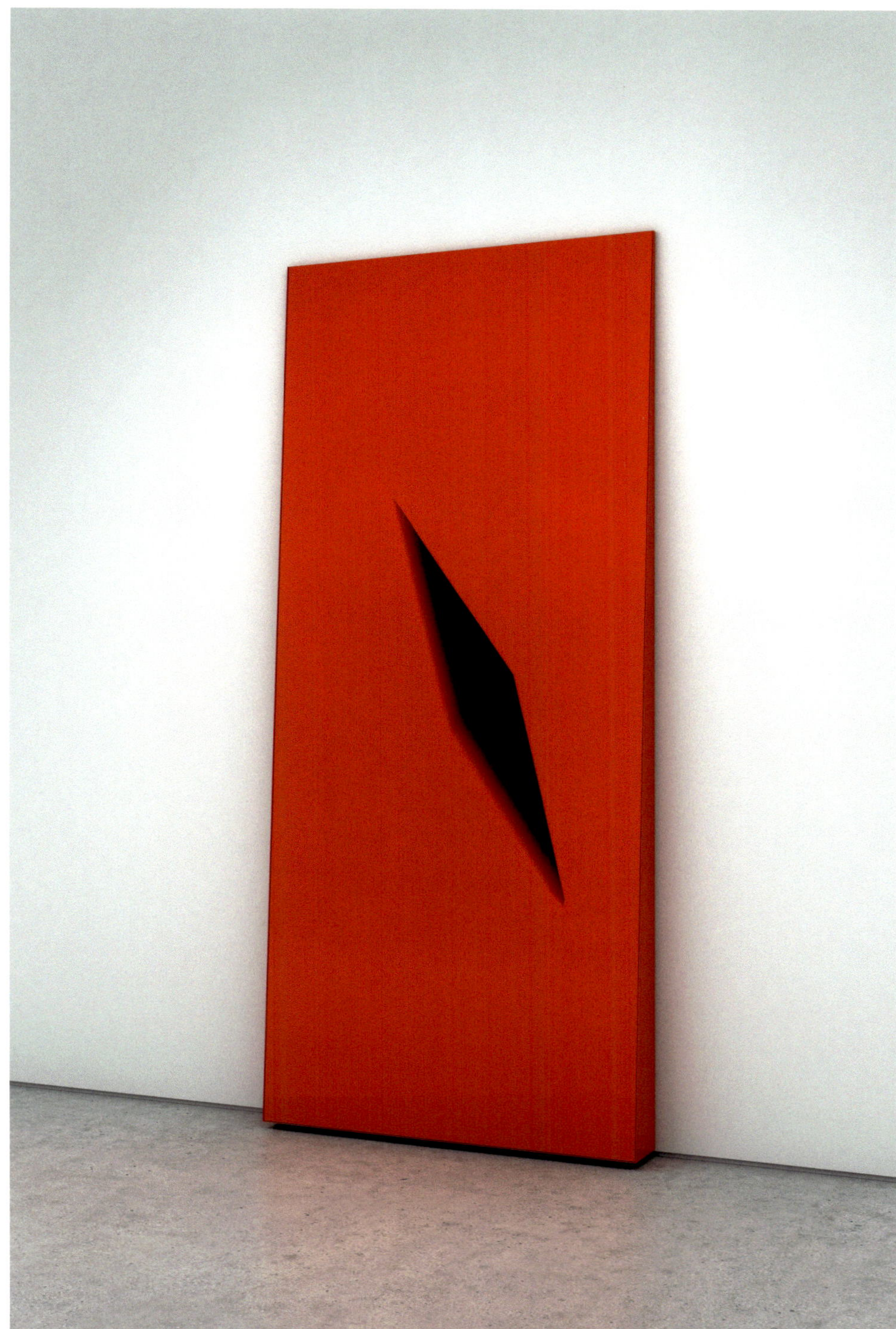

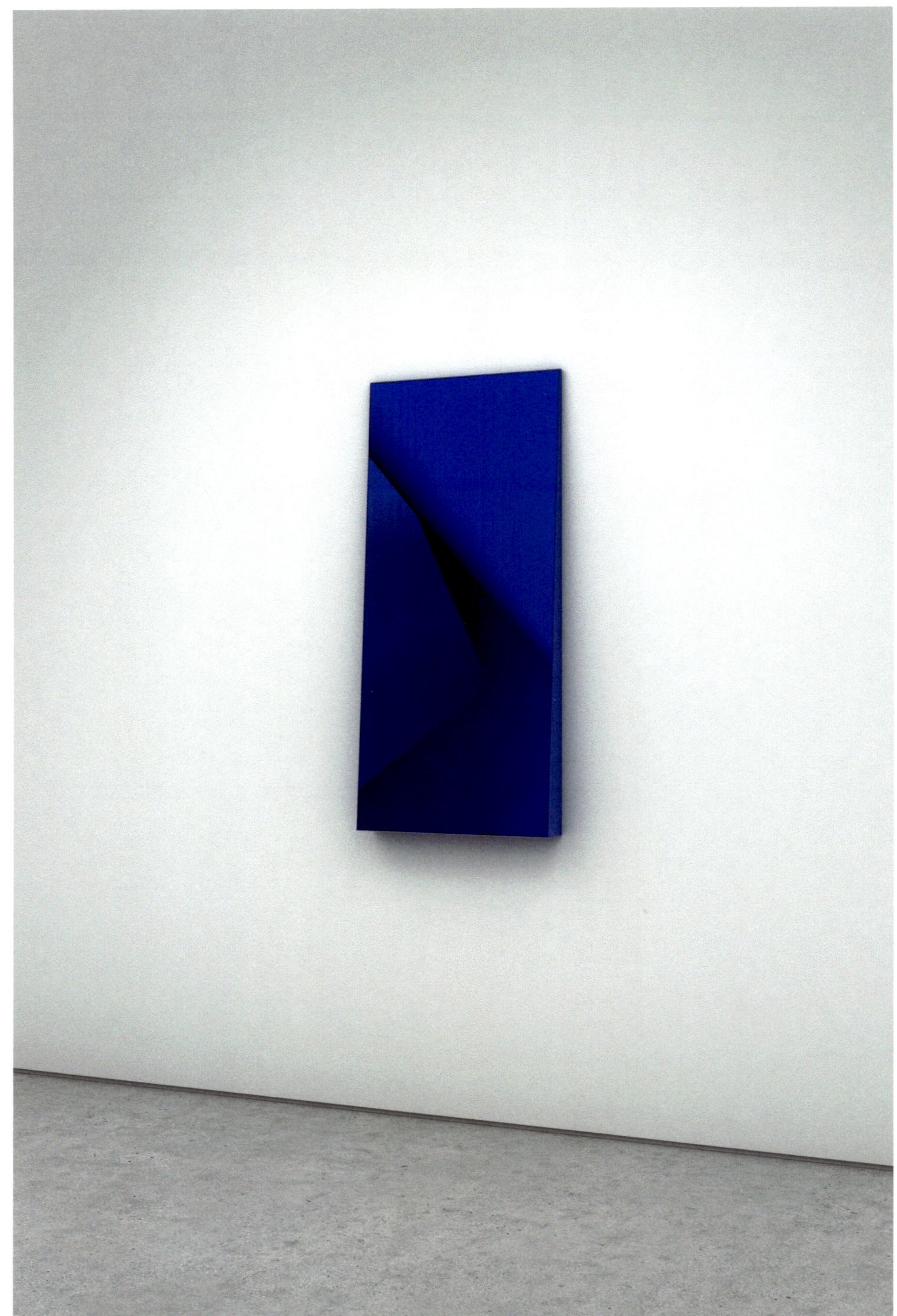

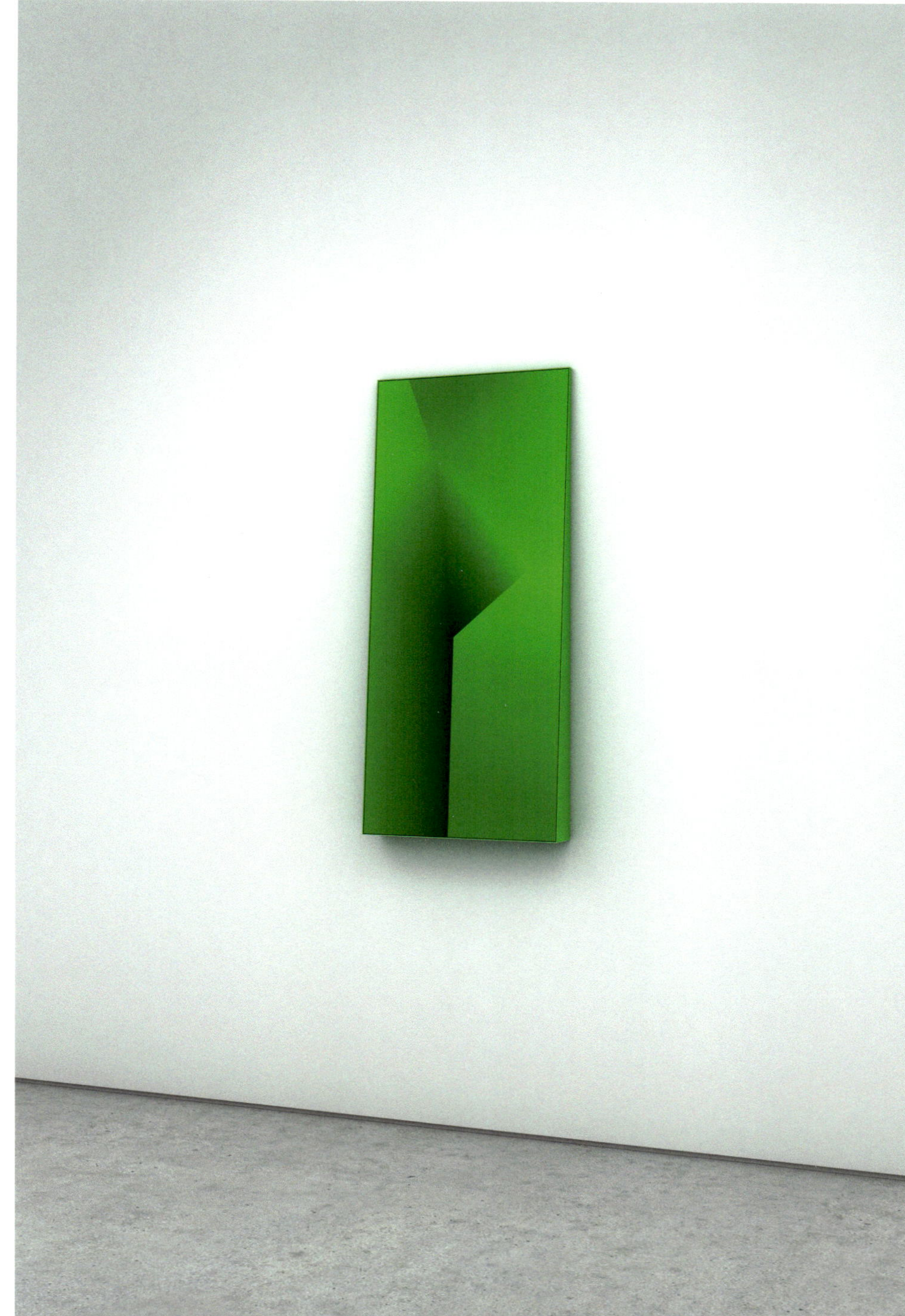

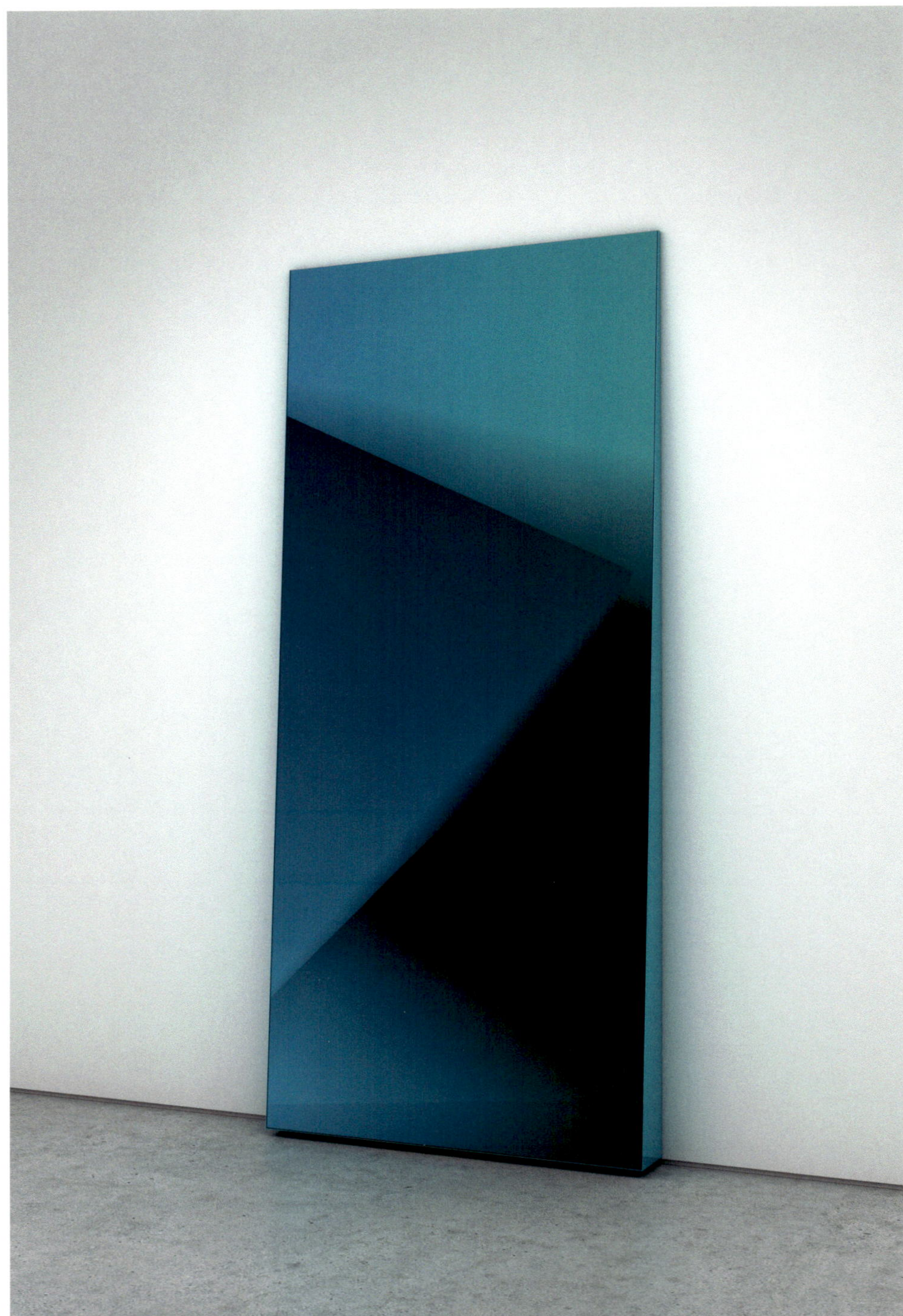

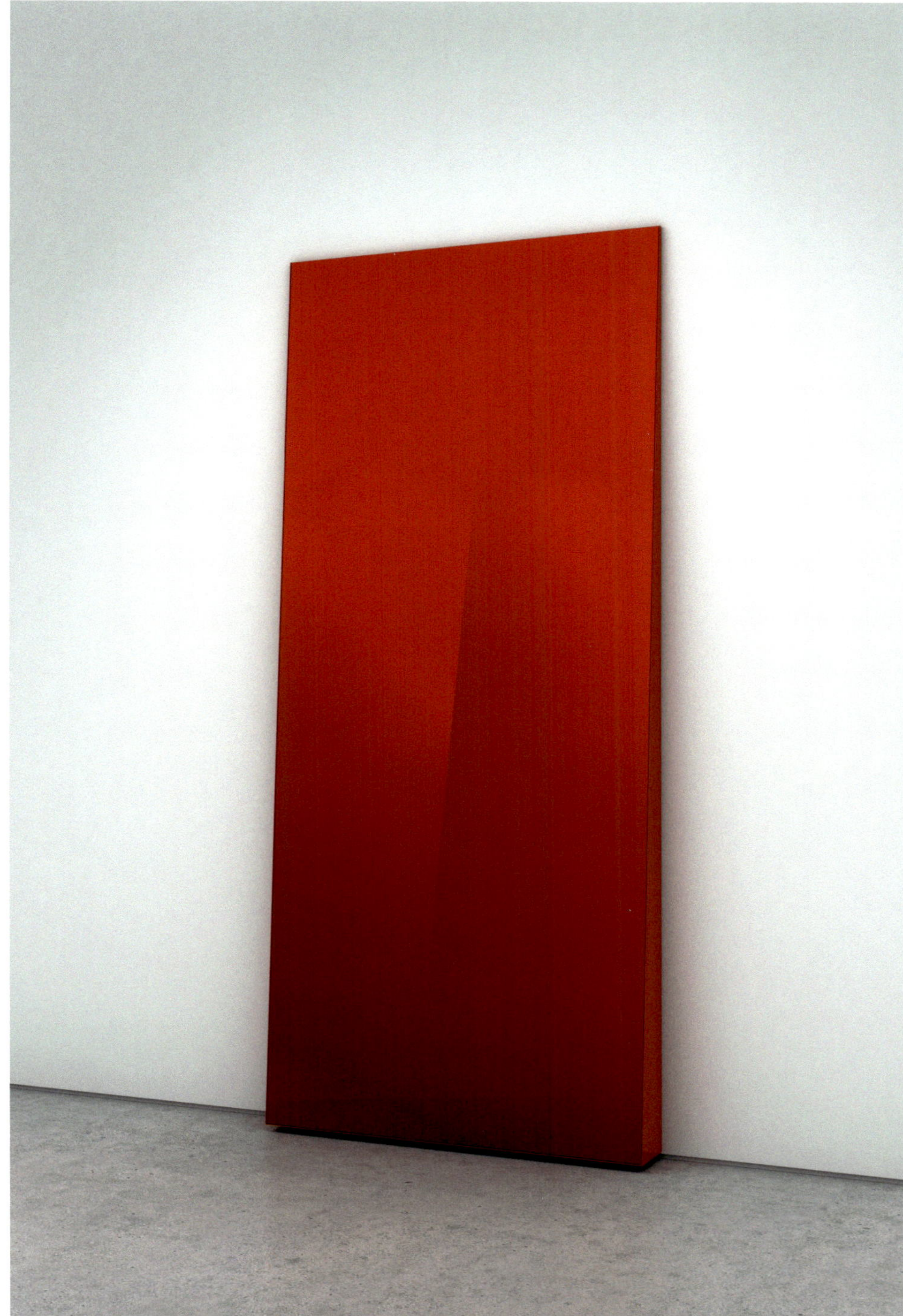

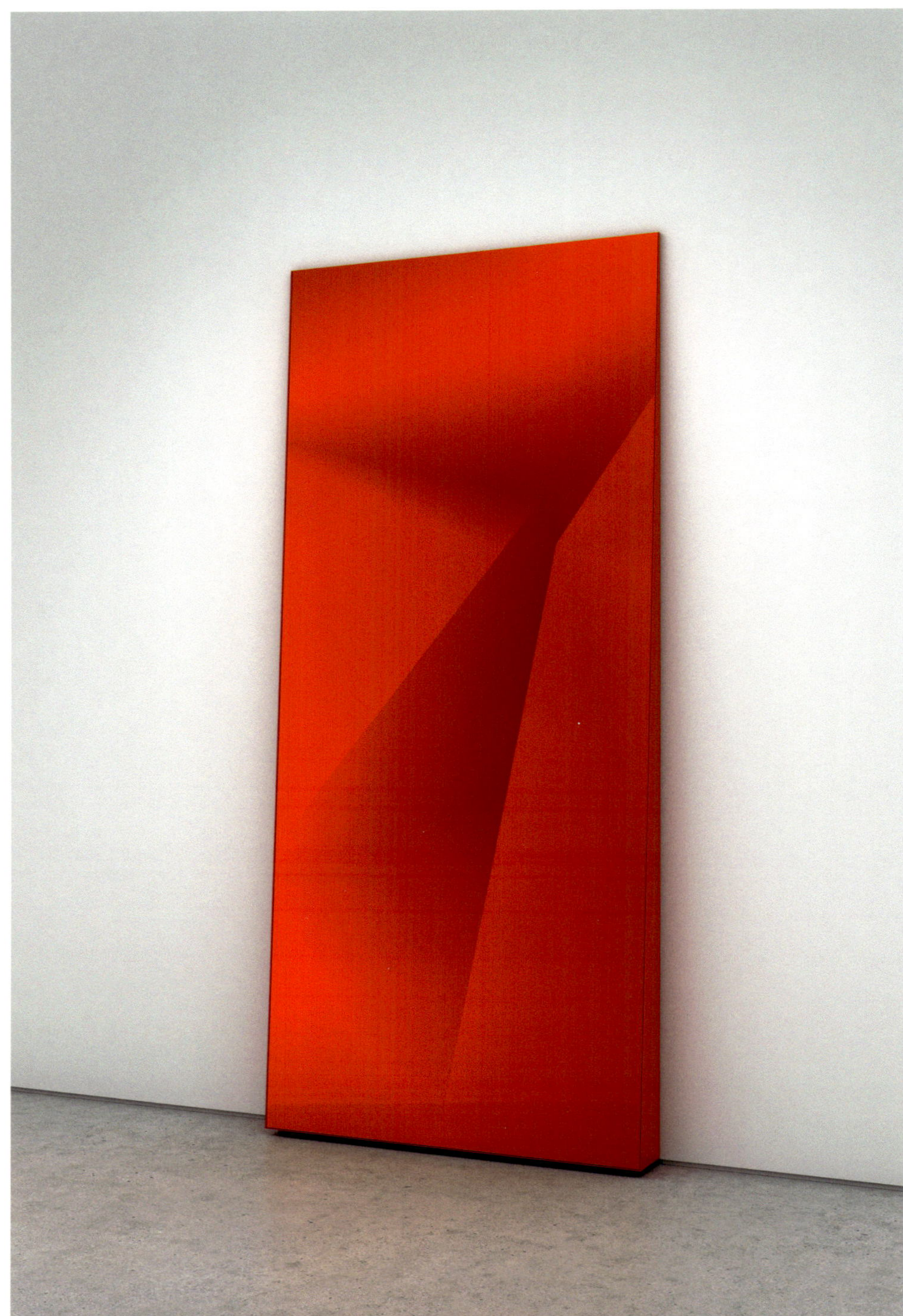

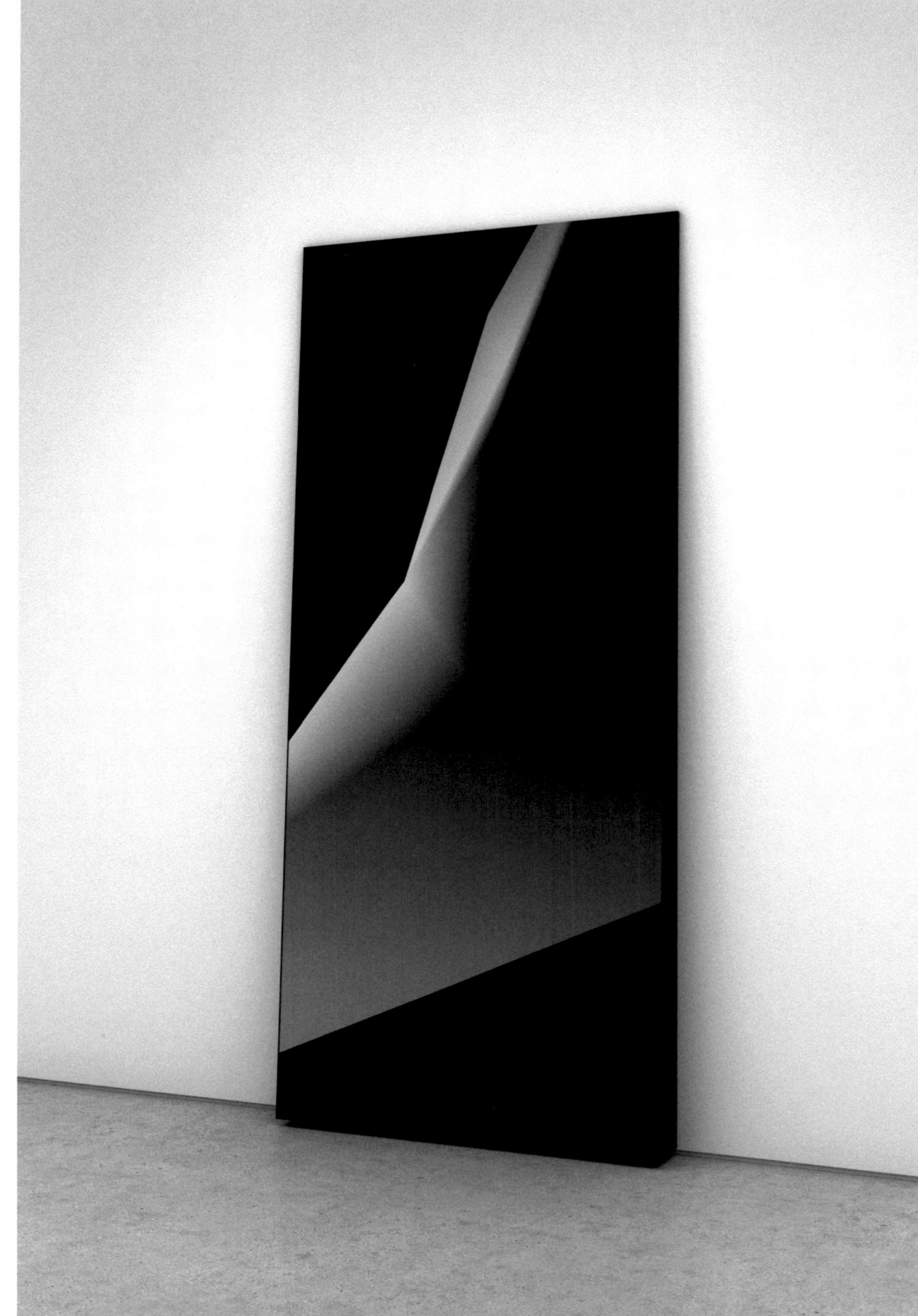

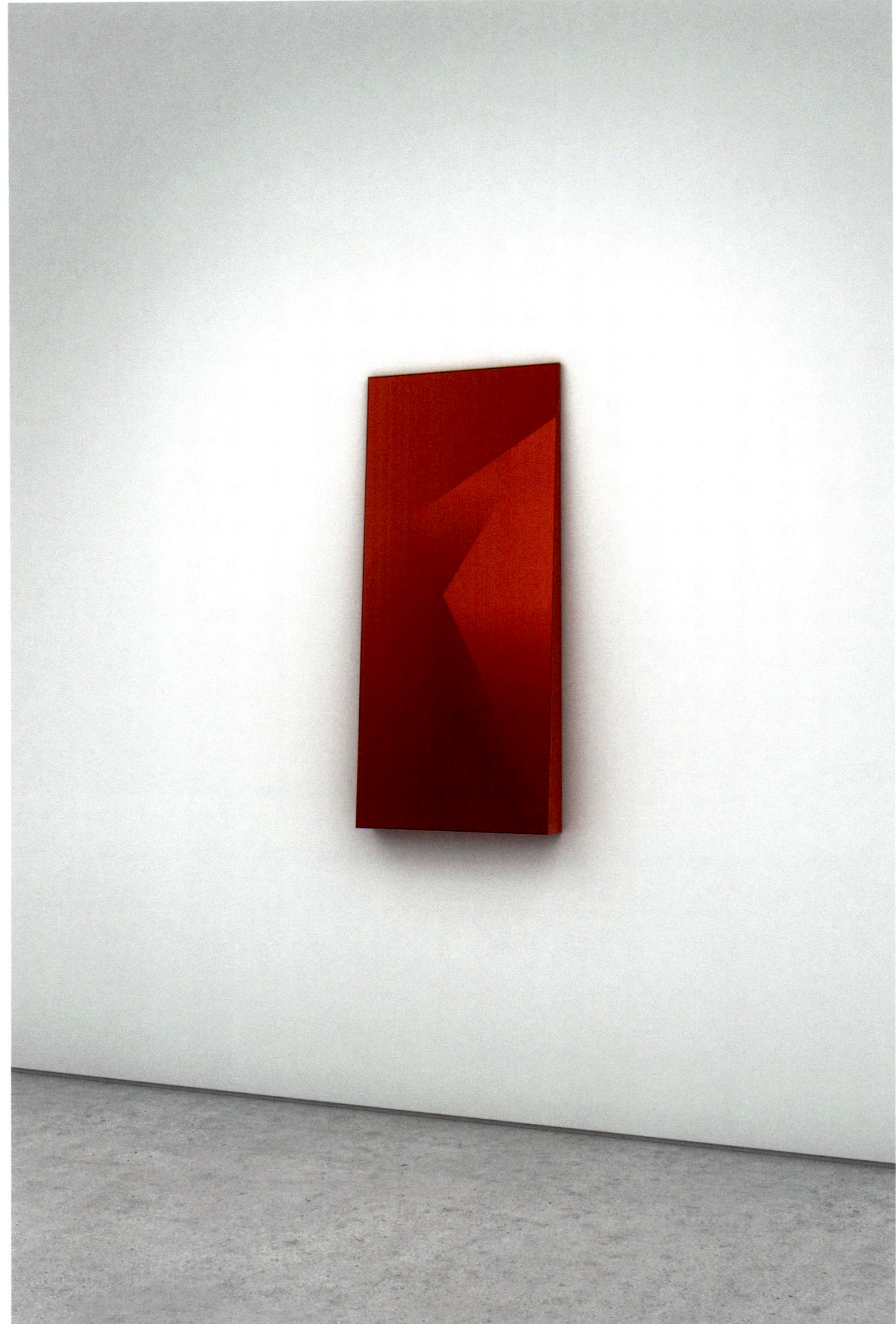

Technical notes & credits

C-type print, UV perspex and aluminium dibond, stainless steel frame

Input data: USGS bare earth digital elevation model (DEM)

No.08 input data: Structure for Motion (SfM) 3D data

Technical advisor: Mark Allan, researcher in geomorphology

No.51, No.161, No.38, No.166,
No.17, No.154, No.105, No.08,
No.184, No.143, No.131, No.126,
Dimensions: 230cm x 105cm, 15cm at base,
closing to 1.2cm at top

No.36, No.259, No.40, No.180,
No.163, No.164, No.201, No.248,
No.270, No.279, No.250, No.280
Dimensions: 121cm x 55cm, 9.5 cm at base,
closing to 1.2cm at top

All works produced 2015 – 2016

Biography

1974 Born in Welwyn Garden City, England, UK

Lives and works in London and Newcastle, UK

Education

1998 BA (Hons) Photography London College of Communication, University of the Arts, London

Selected Solo Exhibtions

2016 A Future Archeology, SCHEUBLEIN + BAK, Zurich, CH
2015 Spatial Objects, Southampton City Art Gallery, UK
2014 Mirrors, Pippy Houldsworth Gallery, London, UK
2012 Transmisson: New Remote Earth Views, NGC, Sunderland; Brancolini Grimaldi, London, both UK
2011 Blackout, Nordin Gallery, Stockholm, SE
and PF Gallery, Poznan, PL
Blackout 10, CIRCA Projects, UK
2010 Blackout, BALTIC Centre for Contemporary Art, Gateshead, UK and Patricia Low Contemporary, Geneva, CH
2007 Ultravisitor, Patricia Low Contemporary, Gstaad, CH
Geographics, Dan Holdsworth + Paul Shepheard, MIMA, UK
White Noise, Store Gallery, London
At The Edge of Space, Parts 1-3, Stills Gallery, Edinburgh, UK
At The Edge of Space, Parts 1-3, National Maritime Museum, Greenwich, London, UK
2005 The Gregorian, Store Gallery, London, UK
2003 Dan Holdsworth, The New Art Gallery Walsall, Walsall, UK
2002 Black Mountains, Entwistle Gallery, London, UK
Dan Holdsworth, Chelsea Kunstraum, Cologne, DE
2001 The World in Itself, Barbican, London, UK
Dan Holdsworth, Kohji Ogura Gallery, Nagoya, JP
Dan Holdsworth, Entwistle Gallery, London, UK

Selected Group Exhibitions

2016 Object-If, DIEHL Berlin, DE
2015 The Idea of Landscape, DZ Bank, ART FOYER, Frankfurt, DE
dark frame / deep field, Breese Little, London, UK
2013 Monuments, Scheublein Fine Art, Zurich, CH
Walk On – 40 Years of Art Walking, NGCA Sunderland, UK
Looking at the View, Tate Britain, London, UK
Landmark: The Fields of Photography, Somerset House, London, UK
2012 Force of Nature: Picturing Ruskin's Landscape, Millennium Gallery, Sheffield, UK
Alaska Editions, Les Douches La Galerie, Paris, FR
Collecting Contemporary Art, Laing Art Gallery, Newcastle, UK
solo-show, Reg Vardy Gallery, Sunderland, UK
2011 Pure Landscape, UBS Art Collection, Tokyo, JP
Shifting Realities: Dan Holdsworth – Michael Reisch, Scheublein Fine Art, Zurich, CH
2010 Questions of Belonging, MIMA, UK
Nuit Blanche, Patricia Low Contemporary, Geneva, CH
CRASH, Homage to JG Ballard, Gagosian Gallery, London, UK

Public Collections

Tate Gallery, London, UK
Centre Pompidou, Paris, FR
mumok, Vienna, A
Victoria & Albert Museum, London, UK
The Government Art Collection, London, UK
DZ Bank Kunstsammlung, Frankfurt, DE
Worchester City Art Gallery, UK
The Saatchi Collection, London, UK
UBS Art Collection, London, UK
Middlesbrough Institute of Modern Art (MIMA), UK
University of the Arts Collection, London, UK
Hackney Museum, London, UK
British Airways Art Collection, UK
Artist Pension Trust Collection, London/New York
The Northern Canon Collection, UK
Sammlung Goetz, Munich, DE
Arts Council Collection, UK
Laing Art Gallery Collection, UK
The Progressive Art Collection, USA
Southampton City Art Gallery, UK

Colophon

Design
Sam Watson

Text
Alistair Robinson

Installation views
EYELEVEL Creative

Production Manager
Sonja Bahr, DISTANZ Verlag

Print
DZA Druckerei zu Altenburg GmbH

Published on the occasion
of the exhibition
Dan Holdsworth
A Future Archeology
June 1 – September 2, 2016

SCHEUBLEIN + BAK, Zurich
www.scheubleinbak.com
info@scheubleinbak.com

Distribution
Gestalten, Berlin
www.gestalten.com
sales@gestalten.com

ISBN 978-3-95476-157-9

Printed in Germany

Published by
DISTANZ Verlag
www.distanz.de

Acknowledgements

Georg Bak, Christina Scheublein, Nicolas Cattelain, Sebastien Montabonel, Tanya Tikhnenko, Sam Watson, Alistair Robinson, Mark Allan, Stuart Dunning, Paul Becker, Dan Matthews, Paul Jarvis, all at Metro Imaging, Phil Brown at O.P.S, Tim Sayler, Thomas Zander, Melanie Vandenbrouck

Edwin Holdsworth, Christine Holdsworth, and Justine & Scarlett

SCHEUBLEIN + BAK